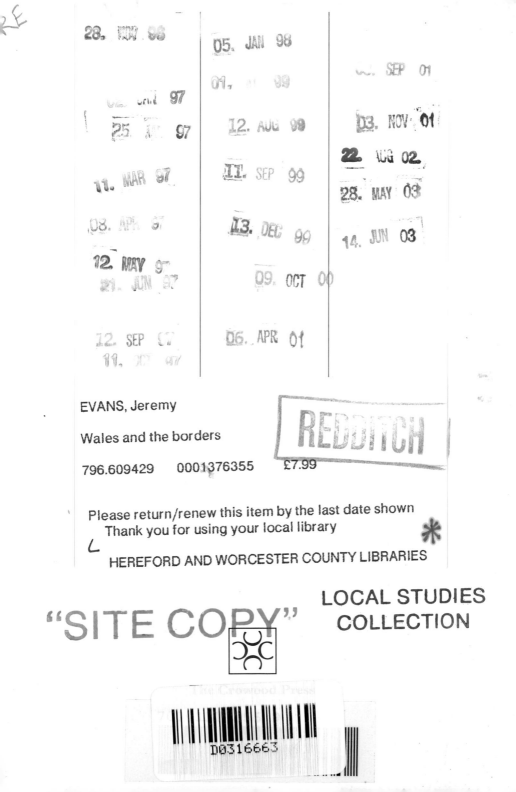

EVANS, Jeremy

Wales and the borders

796.609429   0001376355   £7.99

Please return/renew this item by the last date shown
Thank you for using your local library

HEREFORD AND WORCESTER COUNTY LIBRARIES

The Crowood Press

D0316663

First published in 1996 by
The Crowood Press Ltd
Ramsbury, Marlborough
Wiltshire SN8 2HR

British Library Cataloguing-in-Publication Data
A catalogue record for this book is available from the British Library.

ISBN 1 85223 948 4

Picture Credits
All photographs by Jeremy Evans
Map-drawings by Dave Ayres

Printed and bound by J. W. Arrowsmith Ltd, Bristol

Contents   355

Introduction

RIDE INFORMATION

Area: Where the ride is located.

OS Map: The relevant OS Landranger 1:50,000 map for the route.

Route: Waymarks from start to finish, with OS grid reference numbers. All of the rides in this book are circular, making it possible to start at a number of locations.

Nearest BR Stations: Most of the routes are accessible from a railway station. Check restrictions and costs before you start.

Approx Length: In miles and kilometres. There should always be some allowance for getting lost or altering the route.

Time: This is very difficult to assess, and will depend on factors such as whether the tracks are dry, how many hills have to be climbed, how fast you ride, and how many pubs and places of interest there are en route.

Rating: An 'Easy' ride should be accessible for riders of all abilities, excluding sub-teenage children; a 'Moderate' ride may prove harder in terms of terrain, length, hills, churning those pedals, and possibly navigation; a 'Hard' ride is best suited to experienced offroad riders with a high level of commitment. However these ratings can be changed by the weather – for instance an 'Easy' ride in very dry weather may become a 'Hard' ride when the tracks are churned to mud.

Places to Visit/Pubs and Cafés: Virtually all of these rides feature a number of possible pub and café stops and other attractions.

If you wish to hire a bike, a directory of cycle hire outlets is available free from the Cyclists' Touring Club. Send a large SAE to: CTC, 69 Meadow, Godalming, Surrey, GU7 3HS.

COMMON SENSE OFFROAD

The tracks and trails used for offroad cycling must be shared. The basic problems for mountain bikers is that bikes are generally so much faster than walkers and horse-riders. That is the principal factor which causes antagonism, but why hurry? Why not take it easy and enjoy the ride? Stick to the following common sense rules, and everyone should be happy.

1. Stay on public bridleways, byways or roads. Never ride on footpaths. Cycling on private tracks or open ground is not usually allowed without permission from the landowner. Always moderate your speed.

2. When you ride offroad, the bridleways and byways are classified as 'Highways'. This means the Highway Code applies, and you can be prosecuted for riding dangerously, especially if you are involved in an accident. Any form of racing is illegal on a public highway, unless it is a specially organized event and permission has been obtained. Byways may also be shared with motorized vehicles. They should give way to cyclists, but as when meeting any vehicle, it is necessary to play safe.

3. Learn how to prevent skids and ride with control to help prevent erosion, especially in the wet. If it is very wet, it is much better to push or carry your bike. Going off the official tracks and trails can cause unnecessary erosion, as well as damaging plant and animal environments.

4. When you meet other people offroad and in the countryside, be courteous and considerate. Always slow right down and give way to both walkers and horse-riders, even if it means dismounting and lifting your bike out of the way. Bikes are almost silent, so give warning of your approach in as polite a manner as possible. The British Horse Society would like you to 'Hail a Horse'; we think the very best policy is to come to a complete halt until the animals have passed you by. If you are riding in a group, all go to

one side of the track. Take particular care when you ride past children – you may not worry them, but you may terrorize/infuriate their parents.

5. Make sure your bike is safe to ride, and won't let you down in the middle of nowhere on a fast downhill – learn basic maintenance and take essential spares. In the interests of safety take drink and food, and wear suitable clothing for the weather conditions and length of ride. It is wise to wear a helmet, putting a layer of polystyrene between your cranium and any hard object in the unlikely event of a bad fall.

6. To avoid getting lost, it is always wise to carry a compass and relevant map such as the OS 1:50,000 Landranger series. You should know where you are, and have the ability to re-plan the route and cut the ride short.

7. Follow the Country Code. Leave nothing behind - no litter, no orange peel, the minimum of noise, no bad memories for yourself or for others, and if possible not even a sign of your wheeltracks. Always shut gates behind you (unless they should obviously be left open). Don't blast through fields of cows or sheep - neither they nor the farmer will like it. If you ride with a dog for a companion, keep it under control.

USE THAT MAP!

Unless the route is very easy or you know it well, you should never ride without a map, never ride without a compass. Once you get the hang of it, using them is easy and will ensure you know where you're heading.

A map is a diagram which shows the fea-

Be safe! Don't ride into danger.

tures of an area of land such as mountains, hills, woods, rivers, railways, roads, tracks, towns and buildings. All these and many other features are shown by special signs that map readers can understand. There is always a table on the map which explains the signs. On a 1:50, 000 map (OS Landranger) 1cm on the map equals 50,000cm on the ground; this equals 2cm for every kilometre, or 1^1/4in per mile.

THE GRID SYSTEM: Maps are covered by a grid of numbered horizontal and vertical grid lines. The grid is used to find an exact place on a map. To find a grid reference position you read the first three numbers off the vertical grid line which is called the Eastings line. You then read the next three numbers off the horizontal Northings grid line. Where they meet is where you want to be.

CONTOURS: Contours are lines on a map which join areas that are the same height above sea level (in metres). The difference in height between the contour lines is called the vertical height. The closer the lines are the steeper the hill will be. Contour lines are spaced at 10m intervals on 1:50, 000 Landranger maps, and at 5m intervals on 1:25, 000 Outdoor Leisure maps.

It is generally best to arrange your ride so the climbs are short and steep and the descents are long and fast; it is also best to get major climbs out of the way early on the ride. Sometimes it is quite difficult to know if you will be going up or down; a river or stream on the map is a sure sign of dropping down to a valley, but you can also work it out by looking at the contour line height numbers, as the top of the number is always uphill.

USING A COMPASS: A compass is a valuable aid to finding your way. The most popular style is the Swedish-made Silva on which most modern hiking (equally suitable for biking) compasses are based. It is low in price, light, very tough, and easy to use.

The compass should be carried on a lanyard at all times; in bad visibility it may be the only means you have of finding the way. The compass needle always points to Magnetic North, but keep it away from close contact with any metallic object to which it might be sensitive. Knowing that the needle points North, you can always follow a course in the direction you wish to go. The vertical grid lines on a map point to Grid North; this may be a few degrees different from Magnetic North, but the difference is very small.

OFFROAD WITH KIDS

Why not take the kids with you? With a little care the whole family can have a great day out, and when the kids are too big for a child seat you can put them in the saddle and still stay in control.

There's no point in taking children cycling on-road or offroad if they don't enjoy it, because then you won't enjoy it. Always follow the three golden rules:

1. Make sure they're comfortable.

2. Keep them amused.

3. Don't bite off more than you can chew.

COMFORT: For a child up to around four years of age, go for the best rear-mounted child seat you can find. It must obviously be secure on the bike, with a high back and sides to help protect its occupant if you should fall, deep footwells to protect the feet, and a full harness to hold the child firmly in; a safety bar for the child to grip on to is also a worthwhile extra. Ideally, the seat should also be quick and easy to put on and take off your bike, so when you ride alone the seat doesn't have to go with you.

It's a good idea to get children used to wearing helmets as early as possible, but with very young children (under one year old) there is a often a problem making the helmet stay on. This results in a miserable baby with a helmet tipped down over its eyes; best then to do without the helmet and be extra careful, until you can be sure it will sit comfortably in position.

Make sure the straps of a helmet are sufficiently tight. Children won't like you fiddling under their chins, and your best policy is to train them to put on and take off the helmet themselves as young as possible, ensuring the straps are adjusted to the right length. Shop around for a child helmet and do ask to try it on. As with most adult helmets, removable rubber pads are used to alter the internal diameter, but the most important consideration is that the design of the helmet and its straps hold it firmly on the head. Some helmets seem to want to slide forward on impact, which is useless.

The child is protected from the headwind by your body, but can still get pretty cold sitting there doing nothing; in winter, an all-in-one waterproof/windproof coverall suit does the job really well. Remember that young children require all sorts of extras – extra clothes, nappies, drink, apples, and so on. Try to keep their requirements down to an acceptable minimum; a neat solution is to carry extras in a small backpack that mounts behind the child seat itself.

KEEP THEM HAPPY: Young children generally love riding on the back of bikes, and want to tell you all about what's going on. It can be bad enough understanding them at the best of times, but in this situation it becomes ridiculous and your replies degenerate to a meaningless 'Yes' or 'No'.

With that level of conversation a child will only sit happily in its seat for so long, especially if it's freezing and foul. Children like regular stops if they're to stay happy, so take a stash of little treats – apples, nuts and raisins, and so on – and ensure that you get to the picnic or pub (make sure they allow children) on time with the shortest part of the ride left for the end of the day.

Routes should be chosen with care and an

A child seat can be a lot of fun.

eye on safety. A rock-strewn 'downhill extreme', which is just waiting to throw you over the handlebars, should obviously be avoided. To start with, keep to mellow and easy offroad routes such as those found in the New Forest or an old railway line such as the Downs Link in Sussex. Moderate uphills are all right when the weight of the child helps back wheel traction; immoderate uphills are plain stupid, as you wheeze and groan pushing both bike and child together.

What about downhills? As long as you're in control there's no danger in going fast on a smooth track or road. Rather than hitting the brakes, it's better to treat it as a laugh and teach the child to get used to the thrill of safe speed.

There comes a time when children grow too big and bored for a conventional rear-mounted seat, but too young to ride their own bike and keep pace (and keep safe) with adults. One answer is the Trailerbike, a remarkable hybrid, which claims it will take children from four to ten years old with a maximum weight of 42kg (6.5 stone). It allows you to ride with your child; they get all the fun of riding their own bike, but you have total control over their speed, where they go, and ultimately their safety. They can also pedal as much or as little as they like. If they have the muscle and aptitude, they'll help push you uphill as well as down.

OFFROAD RIGHTS OF WAY IN ENGLAND & WALES

PUBLIC BRIDLEWAYS: Open to walkers and horse-riders, and also to cyclists since 1968. This right is not sacrosanct; bike bans are possible if riders are considered too much of a nuisance.

PUBLIC BYWAYS: Usually unsurfaced tracks open to cyclists, walkers, horse-riders and vehicles which have right of access to houses.

PUBLIC FOOTPATHS: No rights to cycle. You probably have the right to push a bike, but the temptation to ride is high and in general it is best to avoid footpaths whenever possible.

FORESTRY COMMISSION: Access on designated cycle paths, or by permission from the local Forest Manager. At present there is a general presumption in favour of bikes using Forestry land gratis; this may change.

DESIGNATED CYCLE PATHS: Specially built cycle tracks for urban areas; or using Forestry Commission land or disused railway lines. Cycling is illegal on pavements. However it is frequently much safer and more pleasant, and with the proviso that you take great care to avoid pedestrians (who are seldom seen on out-of-town pavements), we suggest that using pavements can be perfectly reasonable.

WHAT IF BRIDLEWAYS & BYWAYS ARE BLOCKED?

Cyclists are used to being on the defensive on Britain's roads; offroad they should stand up for their rights. The relevant landowner and local authority have the responsibility to maintain bridleways and byways and ensure they are passable with gates that work. It is illegal for a landowner to block a right of way, close or divert it (only the local authority or central government can do this), or put up a misleading notice to deter you from using it.

Abide by the rules - never ride on footpaths.

It is also illegal to plough up or disturb the surface of a right of way unless it is a footpath or bridleway running across a field. In that case the farmer must make good the surface within twenty-four hours or two weeks if it is the first disturbance for a particular crop. A bridleway so restored must have a minimum width of two metres, and its line must be clearly apparent on the ground. A farmer also has a duty to prevent any crops other than grass making a right of way difficult to follow. A bridleway across crops should have a two metre clear width; a field edge bridleway should have a clear width of three metres.

If you run into difficulty on any of the above, you can file a complaint with the Footpaths Officer at the local council, giving full details of the offence and a precise map reference.

OFFROAD CARE AND REPAIR

Have you decided on your route, got the right OS map, and your compass? Have you got all the right clothes, ready for rain, wind or sun, plus food and sufficient drink if it's going to be hot? That just leaves your bike so don't risk getting let down by a breakdown...

BRAKE CHECK: The most important part of your bike - if the brakes fail, you could be dead. Check the blocks for wear, turn them or change them as necessary. Lubricate the cables, check they won't slip, and if there is any sign of fraying, change them. Lube the brake pivots – if the spring return on the brakes isn't working well, they will need to be stripped down and cleaned.

WHEELS: Check your tyres for general wear and side-wall damage; look for thorns. If a wheel is out of line or dented, it needs to be adjusted with a spoke key; also check for loose spokes. Always carry a pump and a puncture repair kit.

CHAIN CARE: Give your chain a regular lube – there are all sorts of fancy spray lubes around, some of which cost a lot of money; however, although the more universal sorts are cheap and reliable, they do attract the dirt. If your chain and cogs are manky, clean them with a rag soaked in spray lubricant or a special 'chain bath'; adjust stiff links with a chain breaker.

MOVING PARTS: Clean and lube the derailleur jockey wheels and gear cogs. Lube the freewheel with the bike on its side. Clean and lube the chainwheel gear mechanism. Lube and check the cables for both sets of gears. Lube the bottom bracket – the most basic method is to pour heavy oil down the top tube. Lube the pedals by taking off the end caps. Check that both the cranks and headset are tight. Check that the derailleur lines up properly.

Other things that may go wrong include

Left: Always prepare your bike carefully.

breaking the chain or having a cable slip, though if you take care of your bike these occurrences are very rare. Just in case, however, it is wise to carry a chainlink extrator which rejoins a broken chain, 4/5/6mm Allen keys, a small adjustable spanner, and a screwdriver with both a flat head and a Phillips head. The neat solution is a 'multi-tool' includes all these items in one package.

PUNCTURE REPAIR

The most common offroad repair is a puncture and the most common cause is the hawthorn. To cope with this you need a pump, tyre levers and a puncture repair kit; you may also like to carry a spare tube. Always go for a full size pump with the correct valve fitting; the pump should fit inside the frame, ideally on the down tube. A double action pump puts in the air the fastest. Two tyre levers are sufficient, either in plastic or metal, whilst a spare tube saves the hassle of finding the leak and doing a patch offroad – unless you are unlucky enough to puncture twice.

1. Stop as soon as you feel a tyre go soggy: riding on a flat tyre is asking for trouble. Find a suitable place to do the repair – well away from any cars – and turn the bike upside-down. Take

Mending the tube is usually a quick operation.

care you know where you put things down: it is too easy to lose that little black screw cap that covers the valve.

2. Undo the brake cable near the brake block, flip off the quick release lever at the hub, and remove the wheel. This is more of a fiddle with the back wheel, and it may be necessary to partly unscrew the hub.

3. You won't get the tube out unless it is well deflated. Carefully insert a lever to get the tyre wall off the rim, and then work the rim off all the way round one side using two levers.

4. Pull the tube out of the tyre. The next thing is to find the puncture. Inflate the tube, and then slowly pass it close to your ear and cheek. you should hear or feel the leak and be able to locate it. If this fails, you can try submerging the tube in a puddle and watch for tell-tale bubbles.

5. When you've found the puncture, keep a finger on it so you don't lose it. Roughen the surrounding area with the 'roughener' provided in your repair kit, and then cover the area with a patch sized blob of glue. Now leave the glue to set.

6. To find out what caused the puncture, run your fingers round the inside of the tyre; the probable cause is a thorn which is still in the tyre. Remove it carefully.

7. The glue should now be set enough to put on the patch which should bond straight to the tube. If it seems OK, partly inflate the tube, which makes things easier when getting the tyre back onto the rim.

8. Reassemble the wheel and put it back on the bike. Connecting the brake cable first ensures the wheel is centred by a pull on the brake lever before you tighten the quick release hub; it also ensures you don't ride off with the brake undone. Now inflate the tyre fully.

SAFETY OFFROAD

The first rule of offroad touring is to allow enough time. Getting caught by nightfall is foolhardy and potentially dangerous, particularly if the ride ends in an on-road section and you have no lights. So before you leave, work out how much time to allow, and be pessimistic. Your speed will depend on your skill, level of fitness, and the riding conditions.

Tackling a route after heavy rain in midwinter may take three times as long as the same route in dry summer weather. Riding along a disused railway line will be fast and easy; riding up and down big hills can be exceptionally demanding, and the difference in speed between a good and not so good rider will be much greater.

Riding in a group should ensure some degree of safety, but groups which are much bigger than three riders bring their own problems. They can put an unacceptable load on other people's enjoyment of the environment; walkers and horseriders were there first, and while they can cope with small groups of bike riders, it's no fun for them when a dozen or so Tour de France lookalikes blast through their favourite countryside. By contrast riding alone has much to recommend it; you cause minimum upset to others, and also don't have to worry about keeping up with the fastest member of the group, while the slowest rider doesn't have to worry about keeping up with you.

Whether you ride alone or in a small group, before leaving the golden rule is *tell someone:*
• When you're going.
• When you expect to be back.
• Give them some idea of your route.

It doesn't happen often, but riders do occasionally fall off and knock themselves out or break a few bones in the middle of nowhere; if that happened to you, it would be nice to know that someone would come looking for you, and that they'd be able to locate you before too long.

A First Aid kit is only of value if someone knows how to use it, and even then the constrictions of space and weight on a bike will make its

Don't race unless it's official.

application limited; some bandages and plasters will be enough to deal with minor cuts and abrasions, or possibly support a fracture. In most cases injuries from falls are fairly minor, and you can keep on riding; in more serious cases it will probably be a case of getting help ASAP, while caring for the injured rider:

• If two crash, help the worst injured first.

• If a rider is unconscious, don't leave him on his back. Use the First Aid 'recovery position' if you know how, and cover him with a coat if possible. If a rider is unconscious and not breathing, give the kiss of life if you know how.

• Staunch any bleeding by applying a pad or hand pressure; if bleeding is in an arm or leg, raise the injured limb unless broken.

• Don't move the rider if he seems to be paralysed, unless in immediate danger.

• Don't give the rider anything to eat, drink or smoke.

• Don't leave the injured rider alone.

If you ride regularly it's well worth attending a full length course to get a First Aid certificate which is valid for three years. These are run all round the UK by organizations such as the British Red Cross Society, whose phone number can be found in the local telephone directory.

South Wales –
the Brecon Beacons

There are many possibilities for riding offroad in the southern part of Wales, but if you are looking for the best views and most inspiring terrain the Brecon Beacons National Park is the area to head for. The three rides that follow are all long and can be tailored to give a full day's outing. They should provide a comprehensive impression of the eastern and central areas of the Park, while the more remote western area has considerably fewer offroad routes that are suitable for biking but may still be worth exploring.

Ride 1: The Talgarth Tour

Ride 2: Brecon and 'The Gap'

Ride 3: Sarn Helen Circuit

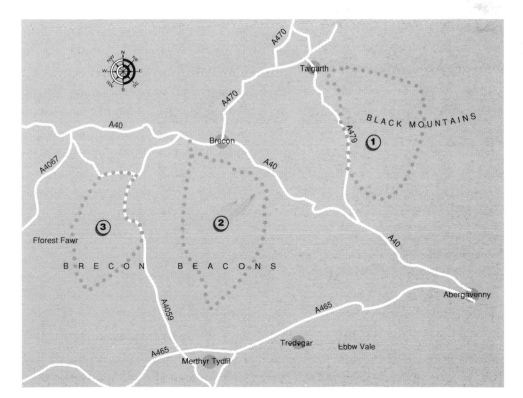

1 The Talgarth Tour

Offroad and On-Road

Area: The Brecon Beacons – a tour of the eastern area. Start and finish at Talgarth on the A49/A4078 east of Brecon. There is a large free car park on the outskirts of the town.

OS Map: Outdoor Leisure 13 – Brecon Beacons – National Park Eastern Area. Landranger 161 – Abergavenny & the Black Mountains.

Route:
Talgarth (GR:154337)
Pengenffordd/A479 (GR:172300)
Rhiw Trumau (GR:190290)
Grwyne Fechan/Hermitage (GR:230251)
Milaid (GR:247220)
Gudder/Llanbedr (GR:245203)
Grwyne Fawr/Partrishow (GR:284226)
Mynydd Du forest (GR:270250)
Grwyne Fawr reservoir (GR:230310)
Y Dâs (GR:200330)
Talgarth (GR:154337)

Nearest BR Station:
None within easy reach.

Nearest Youth Hostel:
Capel-y-ffin to the east of the route at GR:250328.

Approx Length: 52 miles (84km).

Time: Allow about 7 hours, excluding stops.

Rating: Moderate to hard. Conditions are variable but mainly ridable, with some severe uphills.

This circuit has some taxing offroad riding, taking in a couple of the big hills of the Brecon Beacons. A good part of the total distance is on-road, but the roads are mostly so quiet and delightful that riding on them is a pleasure. I originally rode this route clockwise, but came to the conclusion that it would be better to do it anticlockwise, which is the way I have described it. This has the advantage of giving a wonderful offroad downhill from the top of Mynydd Llysiau, though you miss the long on-road downhill through the Mynydd Forest. Whichever way you do it there are some fierce uphills; it is quite a tough marathon, with no distractions from the serious business of riding.

1. From the centre of Talgarth head south on the road signposted to the Mid-Wales Hospital. Follow this minor road all the way to Pengenffordd, joining the main A479 for about 600 yards before forking left onto a byway track just as you come to the woods – if you reach the pub, you have gone too far! Follow the track past buildings at Pant-teg-uchaf, passing more woods on the left and joining a tarmac lane after about half a mile (800m) offroad. Carry straight on ahead here, passing the riding centre and then turning right at a T-junction. A short way on there is a track up to the left, unmarked except for a National Park sign telling you to keep your dog under control as there are sheep about.

2. An optional offroad route to get to here from Talgarth is to follow the byway that skirts the side of the gliding club, and then follow another byway past the remains of the ancient hill fort at Castell Dinas. This is feasible when you are fresh into a ride, but is quite hard and really not rewarding when there is still so far to go.

3. The track is the start of a long uphill up the side of Rhiw Trumau, which for most riders is likely to be a very long push up to the cairn that marks the top at 2,025ft (618m). Do not despair – it is not a good downhill if you are coming in the other direction, and there is a classic to come on the other side. After heading up the rubble-strewn track between trees, the bridleway goes on

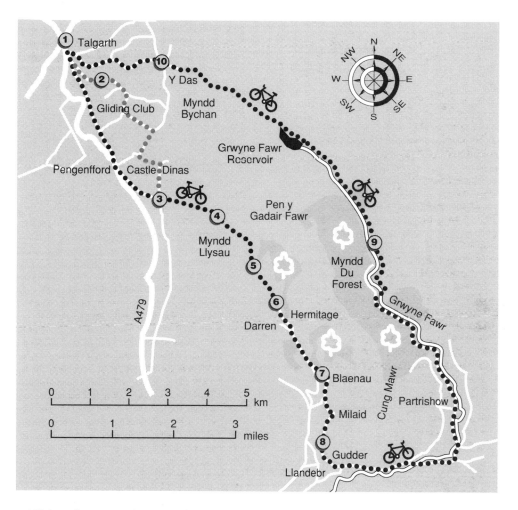

uphill through gates to a sheep pen where it bears right up the side of the hill on a badly eroded but easily followed track. It is steep going here, but the view over the valley to the right below gets better and better as you gain height.

4. Before long you are up at the conspicuous cairn. Turn left to go through the 'gap' that leads over the top here, ignoring the track that heads south-west down the hillside, even though it looks inviting. On the other side of the ridge a rubble-strewn track leads downhill for 100 yards or so before coming to an effective dead end; here you

turn hairpin right to join a really magnificent grass track that heads off along the side of the valley beneath Mynydd Llysiau, steadily losing height on a perfect gradient for easy, fast riding in a magical landscape.

5. Keep on going downhill, drawing level with a great lump of ugly forestry on the opposite hillside that makes the landscape a little less magical. For a time the track becomes really narrow and is slower going as it runs beside a wall, before becoming a grassy track once again as it heads on down to the old stone Tal-y-maes bridge. On the

17

other side of the stream continue to follow the track in much the same direction, with a brief burst of uphill before going through a gate and joining a tarmac track by the side of woods at Tal-y-maes.

6. Carry on down the valley, passing the farmstead at Darren over to the right close by the Hermitage bridge, keeping to the same south-south-east direction and eventually joining the road proper by a bridleway sign marked with a horse insignia. From here on the road is delightful, becoming an old track that can hardly see more than a few cars a year. Past a house with smart gardens on the left, take care to take the left fork downhill, passing a small chapel in an idyllic riverside setting – a grand place for a picnic if no one is about, and no sacrilege as the chapel now serves as part of an outward bound centre.

7. The fairytale road weaves on past a few well hidden houses, bearing right after a house on a corner called Blaenau Isaf, as it heads south with a few ups and downs. Follow the road round to the left as it hooks uphill past Milaid-Isaf, keeping on south to pass a bridleway sign pointing up a track to the left. This bridleway leads steeply uphill and then across wild ground past Blaen-yr-henbant to the Forestry Commission Mynydd Du forest. If you can find the way down past the old disused farmstead at Ffordd-las-fawr it is possible to ride on through the woods to emerge on the road just below Penwyrlod, but as in so many forestry areas bridleways have simply disappeared. Finding the correct route is a nightmare, and I gave up after a wasted hour.

8. It is better to stick to the road, which becomes more of a proper road but still stays quiet as it bears east eventually to reach a multiple crossroads by a solitary telephone box, just above Pontysprig. From here you follow the road going north through the Mynydd Du forest, gradually gaining height as you head through the forestry. This is certainly a good downhill in the other direction, but being on tarmac is comparatively easy to ride uphill. Keep riding up this road, which becomes a byway track as it crosses the river, heading on uphill from the picnic site by the side of the woods. Do not follow the lane along the valley floor here – it leads to the base of the reservoir dam, and there is no way up from there!

9. The byway that continues uphill to the dam at the east end of Grwyne Fawr reservoir is stony but easily ridable. For a brief diversion you can ride across the top of the dam here to check out the view, then carry on following the track by the side of the reservoir, heading out into wilder country on an old road now in a poor state of repair. Keep following this track as it steadily gains height and bears round to the left, becoming muddier and less rocky under your wheels and eventually leading to the top of Y Dâs by a cairn, with splendid views over the landscape to the north-west.

10. From here the track bears right to plunge downhill on a track that is at first too steep and rocky to ride. It zigzags down the hillside and as it drops riding becomes more possible, with the track bearing round to the west to head down towards Wern Frank Wood on a grassy surface – if you think it is tricky coming down, take it from me that it is a swine to go up! Eventually the unmarked route passes between a wide avenue of trees near the bottom of the hill, leading straight ahead to a tarmac lane at Penrhos. Turn right here and then first left, crossing a cattle grid to continue on a quiet lane that brings you rapidly downhill towards Talgarth, passing the Mid-Wales Hospital.

Places To Visit:
Bronllys Castle is about half a mile (800m) to the north-west.

Pubs and Cafés:
No pubs directly on the route, but you could divert to the pub at Llanbedr at the south-west corner of the route, leaving your bike to follow the footpath to cross the river. You may find the combined café and bookshop open in Talgarth.

2 Brecon and 'The Gap'

Offroad and On-Road

Area: The Brecon Beacons – a ride across 'The Gap'. Start and finish at the marketplace car park in Brecon by the Information Centre.

OS Map: OS Outdoor Leisure 11 – Brecon Beacons National Park Central Area. Landranger 160 – Brecon Beacons.

Route:
Brecon (GR:045285)
Bailyhelig road/A40 (GR:037279)
Pont y Caniedydd/Nant Sere (GR:039245)
Fan y Big (GR:032205)
Taf Fechan forest (GR:035173)
Pentwyn and Pontsticill Reservoirs (GR:054144)
Pen Bwlch Glasgwm (GR:090161)
Talybont reservoir (GR:105190)
Talybont-on-Usk (GR:116225)
Pencelli (GR:093250)
Llanfrynach (GR:076257)
Brecon (GR:045285)

Nearest BR Station:
None within easy reach.

Nearest Youth Hostel:
Ty'n-y-Caeau accessible by the bridleway Slwch Lane running due east from Brecon at GR:074388.

Approx Length: 30 miles (48km).

Time: Allow around 5 hours, excluding stops.

Rating: Moderate. Mainly good tracks and reasonably straightforward navigation. You go high, but it is steady climbing.

This is a ride with brilliant views and some very good tracks, heading through the centre of one of Britain's most attractive National Parks. The people are also very friendly. An elderly Brecon local pointed out 'The Gap', which allows you to cross the pass between the two big peaks of Cribyn and Fan y Big, going into rapturous detail about the offroad route that he used to ride on his motorbike some thirty years previously. The Roman road that leads up to 'The Gap' has deteriorated in the meantime, but is still ridable nearly all the way as you set out on this excellent circuit.

1.   Market day in Brecon is Tuesday, when the marketplace should be avoided unless you want to trade in sheep. Otherwise it is usually pretty empty, and is a good place to start this ride from. Before leaving you may wish to check out the Information Centre, which sells relevant maps and other publications.

2.   Ride through Brecon, following the Cardiff direction out of town. This takes you over the bridge across the River Usk. A short way on past traffic lights, turn left by a small church down the Bailyhelig road, which is unmarked except for a signpost pointing to the Hospital. Ride on past the hospital, heading uphill on-road and across the dual carriageway A40. Keep following the road on a moderately steep uphill heading due south, passing a large farm at Bailyhelig and some way on passing a bed and breakfast place at Twyn with fine views of 'The Gap' ahead of you – it looks intimidating from down here, but is not too bad.

3.   Farther on the road bends left downhill. Take the next turning on the right (marked as a byway on the OS map), heading on downhill across the Nant Sere river, following the tarmac lane as far as a gate, by a track going down to the left to Cwmcynwyn Farmhouse. Go straight through this gate ahead, starting the long ascent up the side of Bryn Teg on a rough track. At the next gate by a National Trust sign you go into open sheep grazing country, following the track uphill and ignoring a narrow track that bears off

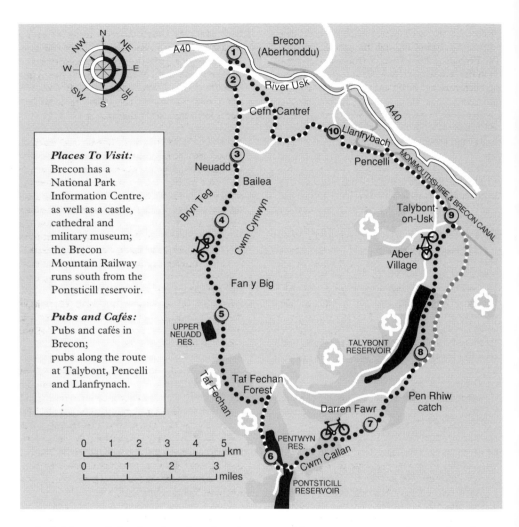

Places To Visit:
Brecon has a National Park Information Centre, as well as a castle, cathedral and military museum; the Brecon Mountain Railway runs south from the Pontsticill reservoir.

Pubs and Cafés:
Pubs and cafés in Brecon; pubs along the route at Talybont, Pencelli and Llanfrynach.

to the left by a wall, heading down into the valley. Keep on up the main track, which is an old Roman road, with a surface that gets rockier as you gain height but is mainly ridable. The track leads straight up to 'The Gap' between Cribyn and Fan y Big – for walkers there is a mighty natural horseshoe here extending to Pen y Fan, which makes a fine ridge walk.

4. As you get higher the track is likely to get wetter, and at times is like riding up a stream. Towards the top the track bears round to the left

and becomes steeper up rock steps, the only part so far that is unridable. Go on through 'The Gap', taking in the fine view behind before heading off on a long, steady downhill going south on a fairly good surface. Upper Neuadd reservoir is passed down on the right; at the southern end of the reservoir the track dips steeply down and up to cross a crevasse by Filter House, before going through a gate and following the track by the side of the woods ahead.

5. Keep on along the track until you reach the

road at Taf Fechan Forest. Follow the quiet lane on a fast downhill through the woods, crossing Taf Fechan at Pont Cwmyfedwen and carrying on in the same direction. Keep straight on, ignoring a left turning, with Pentwyn reservoir coming into view on the left. More downhill brings you past a solitary converted chapel, with a parking and picnic place on the left, which is a good spot to stop and check the map and have some lunch.

6. A short way past here, take the turning that doubles back to the left, crossing between the Pentwyn and Pontsticill Reservoirs. Keep on the lane ahead, passing the Dolygaer Outdoor Pursuits Centre, as you head uphill going east-north-east. The lane turns into a rough track, steadily gaining height on a variable surface before passing through a gate at the end of the woods. There are no signposts, so follow the most obvious track, which bears off to the right here, before resuming the east-north-east direction across open country. This route eventually brings you up to 1,700ft (520m), bearing left to the north through the Pen Bwlch pass with brilliant views of the Dyffryn valley down to the right.

7. From here on the riding is really excellent, as the big Talybont reservoir opens out ahead. Follow this fine, fast track towards the forestry. Just before you reach it, a track bears left downhill by a ruined building, a turning that is easily missed. This is the offroad route to Talybont; if you miss the turn you will come to a gate, with the track running on ahead by the side of the forestry. From here it becomes a road heading on a long, long downhill towards Talybont; you are unlikely to meet many cars, so this route can be equally enjoyable.

8. The offroad route is, however, superb. Head downhill from the ruined building, and where the track forks left and right take care to go right, following a narrow, fast track along the contour line of the hillside, going through thick forest with the reservoir far below to the left. The track soon passes above the northern end of the reservoir, carrying on through the woods as it takes you on a bumpy downhill towards Talybont. A short

way before the village the track turns left over a disused railway bridge to cross the old line, bringing you past the Monmouthshire and Brecon Canal to the White Hart pub – this is in a pleasant position with canal boats gliding by, and is the first pub on the ride, some three to four hours from the start at Brecon.

9. From here it is mainly on-road back to Brecon, but most of the roads are narrow country lanes where you seldom see cars, so it is still enjoyable riding. Turn left through Talybont where there is another pub, following the road for just over two miles (3km) to Pencelli, which also has a pub. From here you could follow the road to join the main A40 into Brecon – acceptable if you are in a hurry, but I would recommend a quieter option. Turn left by the telephone box in the middle of Pencelli, going up a short track to cross the bridge over the canal. Turn right along the lane here, and follow it all the way to the next village, which is Llanfrynach, the only place I saw any cars on this part of the ride – and they were parked.

10. Make for the church in Llanfrynach – there is a pub here too – turning left and left again for Cantref. Follow the pretty lane for a mile or so by the side of Afon Cynrig, riding uphill by Cantref Church, which is hidden in trees with some attractive large houses on the way. Past here ignore the left turn signposted to Brecon, bearing right and then following the road past the modernised farmhouse at Tir-y-groes with a conspicuous footpath sign opposite.

11. Keep on along the lane until it turns sharp left with a track going straight ahead. Follow this track, which is the last offroad section of the ride, into Brecon, heading on a bumpy downhill before crossing the A40 and bearing left to come out opposite the hospital on the Bailyhelig road. Take care here; there is no obvious place to stop and cars from the hospital can whiz by unexpectedly. From here turn right and retrace your tracks on-road back into Brecon, which boasts a bike shop even if it has few inspiring places for tea.

3 Sarn Helen Circuit

Offroad and On-Road

Area: The Brecon Beacons – a tour of the central area. Start and finish at the Brecon Beacons Mountain Centre, to the south-west of Brecon off the A470.

OS Map: Outdoor Leisure 11 – Brecon Beacons National Park Central Area. Landranger 160 – Brecon Beacons.

Route:
Brecon Beacons Mountain Centre (GR:977262)
Ffynon-ynys-gron/A4215 (GR:967248)
Sarn Helen Roman road (GR:937210)
Plas-y-gors/Blaen Llia (GR:927160)
Ystradfellte (GR:930133)
Penderyn/A4059 (GR:948089)
Llwyn-on reservoir (GR:003120)
Garwnant Forest Centre (GR:003132)
Pont Llysiog/A470 (GR:005142)
Storey Arms Outdoor Education Centre/A470 (GR:983203)
Glyn Tarell (GR:980232)
A4215/A470 (GR:988248)
Libanus (GR:993257)
Brecon Beacons Mountain Centre (GR:977262)

Nearest BR Station: None within easy reach.

Nearest Youth Hostel:
Ystradfellte at GR:925127.
Llwyn-y-celyn at GR:993939.

Approx Length: 30 miles (48km).

Time: Allow around 5 hours, excluding stops.

Rating: Easy. Mainly good tracks. Navigation through forestry from Garwnant Forest Centre is tricky.

This is a fine circuit round the central area of the Brecon Beacons. There is a fair amount of on-road, but apart from an unpleasant stint on the A470 this is all enjoyable riding, and there are excellent offroad sections along the ancient Roman road of Sarn Helen and the drovers' road on the side of the Glyn Tarell Valley.

1. The Brecon Beacons Mountain Centre is a good place to start and finish this ride. If you come by car there is plenty of parking space, and inside the building you will find books, maps and an information centre with helpful staff; downstairs there is a café and picnic area with outside seating and really fine views across to the mountains, with a garden that is a good place for children to play in. Alternatively you could start this ride from Brecon itself, making your way to the Mountain Centre by minor roads and a final stretch of bridleway, adding some 5 miles (8km) to the total distance.

2. Turn left out of the Mountain Centre, keeping left along the side of the woods and following a track over open grassland, which is comparatively easy going. This brings you to the road ahead at Fynnon-ynys-gron. Go straight over here and along the lane ahead, riding through the gate by Forest Lodge Cottages and joining Sarn Helen, the old Roman road. This is mainly excellent riding and very easy to follow, skirting the side of the mountains as it passes Forestry Commission woods on the right.

3. The track bends round in a loop, following a fine avenue of hawthorns that are ablaze with red berries in the autumn. Swinging round to the south the track climbs uphill for a while, before bending left a dropping downhill to Pont Blaen-cwm-du, a fine place with stark hills on the left and rolling valleys away to the right. The track bears sharp left over a bridge here, heading uphill on a rough surface that is more like a river in flood after heavy rain – it is interesting to ride, though you will be excused for a little pushing.
   At the top the track continues to follow the contours of the hillside on a good surface in a

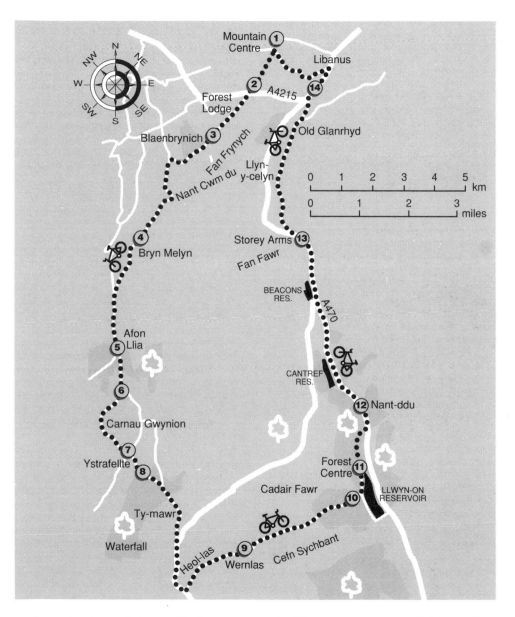

magical setting, though during my ride there was water everywhere, nowhere more so than when crossing the waterfall marked on the OS map – this proved a tricky place to stay dry.

4. After some more easy climbing to Bryn Melyn, the Sarn Helen track keeps straight on to join a quiet road just past Rhyd Uchaf, ending a fine start to this ride. Head south along the road, which is a biker's delight – straight, more down-

Within easy reach of the Brecon Beacons Mountain Centre, this stretch of Sarn Helen offers a lovely ride with a steady climb towards Bryn Melyn.

hill than up, and when I rode it only a shepherd's Land Rover and a car parked by the verge were there to remind me that the world of automobiles existed. The road continues through a wild landscape, following the course of the Afon Llia on the left and then passing a cattle grid and entering forestry, where a track off to the right is the continuation of Sarn Helen.

5. From here Sarn Helen goes all the way to Neath, which apparently is a fine ride, except that the return involves a lot of on-road riding. I had toyed with the idea of following Sarn Helen round to the edge of the Coed y Rhaiadr forestry, where the OS map shows a connecting bridleway heading eastwards through the woods to rejoin the road. This was discounted in favour of staying on the road – as advised by the warden at the Mountain Centre, who said I would definitely get lost in the forest.

6. Keep on south along the road past the forestry with its marked picnic area. A short way on, the road bends sharply left on a downhill, and here you go straight ahead up a track, shown as byway on the OS map though signposted as a footpath. Follow this round to the right on a grassy surface heading up between dry stone walls. After an easy uphill the track swings left between the twin rock outcrops of Carnau Gwynion, which have old mine workings in their sides, heading on through a gate and then bearing left (do not take the less obvious track going

straight ahead) across heath and rock pillow mounds. This brings you down to a gate in a very muddy corner of a field, and then to an overgrown grassy track that heads downhill into the small hamlet of Ystradfellte.

7. After around two hours' riding I was delighted to reach this place at 1pm, looking forward to visiting the pub clearly marked on the OS map. However when I arrived the pub was closed, and looked like it had been closed for some time! Ystradfellte is also a famous centre for exploring the half dozen or so Brecon Beacons waterfalls – they are all located to the south, and can be found with an OS map, but must be approached on foot.

8. To continue the ride, follow the road past the church and over the Afon Dringarth, and head steeply uphill before the road levels out with a series of easy ups and downs through more forestry. Coming once again into open country, this quiet road then starts a fast downhill, passing Ty-mawr and crossing the Hepste bridge to join the main A4059. Turn right onto this road for about a mile – there is little traffic, and it is mainly downhill into Penderyn, which gets it over quickly. Here there is a pub in an uninspiring setting if you want to stop; just opposite the pub you turn left onto a narrow lane with a rusty old sign pointing to Cwm Cadlan.

9. This is another really quiet road – just one car and one lorry passed me in 4 miles (6.5km) or so. It goes steadily uphill past the cattle grid to cross open moor, before heading rapidly downhill through forestry to reach the Llwyn-on reservoir, a great ride on a deserted road. When you come to the crossing road that runs along the side of the reservoir, a short path leads down to the 'beach' here, a pleasant spot to stop on a fine day if the water is not too high.

10. To continue turn left (north) along the road, which is also extremely quiet. After just under a mile you come to a turning signposted to the Garwnant Forest Centre, and have the option of keeping along the road to join the A470 or turning off for a ride through the woods. The Forest

Fabulous scenery is the norm for this corner of Wales. If you ride it at the right time, you'll also have most of the countryside to yourself.

Wales can be a soggy place on occasions, and if undertaking a long ride of this kind in winter it's well worth guarding against cold, wet feet.

Centre here could be worth a visit, though it was closed when I called by. The picnic area is good, and there is an impressive range of outdoor activities for children.

11. The straightforward route is to follow the road to the A470. An option is to find the clear track that heads north past the Garwnant Forest Centre to the ruins of Wern Farm in the midst of the woods. This can be followed for about a mile until it meets a bridleway, where you turn right at Valve House, and then right again to cross the reservoir dam to the A470 at the southern end of the Cantref reservoir.

12. Unfortunately the A470 is the only way to continue north. It is a fairly busy road, and since it is mainly uphill it takes a comparatively long time to cover the 3 miles (5km) or so that are required. However, it is not too bad and you soon go offroad again! The turn-off to look out for is on the right, just after a stretch of woodland where the road swings left past a parking place. On the opposite side of the road there is an isolated white building that is the Storey Arms Outdoor Education Centre; you will find the start of the track by the public telephone box.

13. Ignore the gate on the right, which is a footpath, and follow the track ahead along the side of the valley, which is the old drovers' road. At first this runs parallel to the road on a great downhill section, before bearing off to the right and getting well away from the road on the opposite hillside. The riding along the partly walled track is delightful, and all too soon you hit tarmac at Blaenglyn Farm, though it is still a bridleway. The Youth Hostel is down in the valley here, but unfortunately must be approached from the main A470.

14. The bridleway leads to the road at Old Glanrhyd. If you want to go to Brecon, turn right here and follow the quiet country lanes for 5 miles (8km) or so to the town. For the Mountain Centre turn left, which brings you back onto the A470, though this time it is downhill and in no more than five minutes you reach Libanus where the sharp left turning for the Mountain Centre is clearly signposted. From here it is a steady climb on a quiet country road, which after 10 minutes or so of pedalling should bring you up to the common called Bedd Gwyl Illtyd. If you have made it in time turn right over the cattle grid for a wel-come cup of tea at the Mountain Centre, a very pleasant place to sit and mull over the delights of this ride.

Places To Visit:
Brecon Beacons Mountain Centre has a car park, café, information centre and picnic area.

Pubs and Cafés:
Pubs at Ystradfellte and Penderyn.

Mid Wales and the Borders

Mid Wales and the nearby border country offer a wealth of offroad potential combined with some of the quietest, most enjoyable country lanes you can imagine. The eleven rides that follow only touch on the possibilities in this area, but provide a good spread of terrain and scenery – ranging from the wildness of the Elan Valley in the west, via the border country of the Kerry Ridgeway, to the homely delights of Wenlock Edge in England.

4 The Elan Valley

**Offroad and
On-Road**

Area: Mid Wales – a tour of the Elan
Valley. Start and finish at Rhayader.
Alternatively if arriving by car you can
start and finish at car park just past Elan
Village on the B4518 road 3 miles (5km)
south-west of Rhayader at GR:923645.

OS Map: Landranger 147 – Elan Valley
& Builth Wells area.

Route:
Rhayader (GR:970680)
Caban-coch reservoir car park (GR:923645)
Claerwen reservoir car park (GR:872634)
Claerwen (GR:823672)
Clawdd Du Mawr (GR:856695)
Carn Ricet (GR:872709)
Rhosmeheryn (GR:897716)
Penygarreg reservoir car park
(GR:915673)
Caban-coch reservoir car park
(GR:923645)
Rhayader (GR:970680)

Nearest BR Station:
Llandrindod Wells.

Nearest Youth Hostel:
Dolgoch to the south-west of the route
at GR:806561.

Approx Length: 27 miles (43km).

Time: Allow 4 to 5 hours.

Rating: Moderate. Most of the ride is
easy, but parts of the Ancient Road are
tricky and you can go off the trail.

*We rode this circuit on a spectacularly cold
and clear day in December, when the roads
and tracks were completely clear and we
met scarcely a soul on the way. However,
you can imagine lots of cars crawling round
these narrow roads in summer! The route
divides into three sections – an enjoyable
on-road to start; a long and quite tricky
offroad section along an Ancient Road; and
another enjoyable and very fast on-road to
finish. The Ancient Road crosses open moor
and is exposed to all weather. In winter it is
liable to be wet, boggy and comparatively
slow going; and it is not too difficult to
wander off the trail and get lost. There
should be no problems during a fine summer, but it is not a good place to be caught
at nightfall at less forgiving times of the
year!*

1. From Rhayader follow the B4518 signposted
to Elan Village. After 3 miles (5km) or so, you
pass the left turning down to Elan Village with its
large Information Centre, which ap-pears to be
closed throughout the winter. Just after this turning you come to the first big dam on the left,
with a free car park beneath the cliffs opposite. If
you have come this far by car, leave it here and
start the ride.

2. Follow the road on round to the right, and
then turn left over the bridge with its spectacular
copper cupolas – you cannot imagine modern
water companies going to such splendid excess in
these days of profit and austerity. Turn left on
the far side of the bridge and follow the road
round the north side of the Caban-coch reservoir, which is extremely pleasant riding when
there are no cars to bother you. Keep on following the road past the solitary, incongruous telephone box, heading on a steady uphill past the
big farmstead at Ciloerwynt.

3. A short way past here fork off to the right on
a higher road that brings you up to the top of the
magnificent Cerrigcwplau dam by a noticeboard,
where you go offroad. Follow the track ahead
round the edge of the Claerwen reservoir, which
is easy riding with the mildest of uphills and

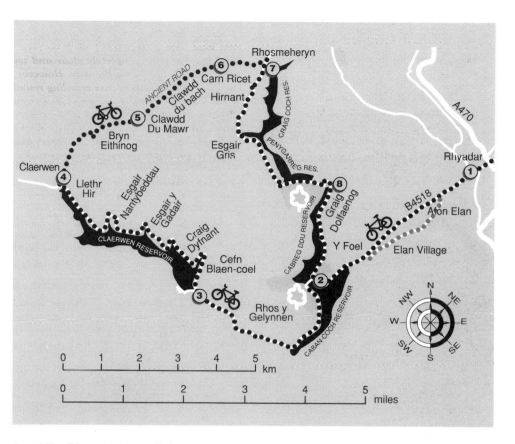

downhills. The track leads all the way to the north-west end of the reservoir.

4. Just past here you come to the solitary farmstead of Claerwen on the hillside to the right, while the track bears left and comes to a bridge with a padlocked gate, though as it happens this is bridleway. However this is not the way to go. You want to turn up the hill before reaching the farm, to connect with the 'Ancient Road' that leads north-eastwards across the moors. The vague semblance of a track going up the steep hillside is about 250 yards east of the Claerwen farmstead – push up the grassy slope to the top of Esgair Cywion, aiming to head along the top of the highest hill where you will find a wide grass track that eventually joins the Ancient Road.

5. At first this is an easily followed track, dropping down and then up round the right side of the crags at Cnapyn Blaendrawsffos. From here the track carries on in a north-north-west direction and is easily followed, except at one point where it bears down the left side of a bluff at Clawdd Du Mawr, and appears to fork right and left into two tracks. The right track goes uphill, and looks the most obvious way to go since it is worn by four-wheel-drive vehicles; the left track is very indistinct and grassy, but is the correct way to go. It eventually becomes easier to follow along the ridge of Clawdd-du-bach, while the other track simply leads to nowhere.

The other problems when navigating the Ancient Road are water and bogs. Some parts of the track disappear under water; you do not realize how deep it is until you attempt to ride

Which way now? The Elan Valley Reservoirs are popular spots in high season, and offer the chance of a truly memorable bike ride which takes most of a day.

They don't build them like that any more! Modern water companies are mere cheapskates compared to the magnificent Victorians.

through and end up with soaking feet – no problem in the summer, but bad news in the winter when there is still a long way to go. The track also crosses numerous bogs. Some are firm enough to ride or push through; others are so soft that you can sink down to your thighs in no time, getting very cold and muddy in the process.

6. At the top of Carn Ricet, one of the highest points of the ride, a weather station comes into view on the right. From here the going becomes much easier, with the clearly defined track swooping down across grassland on a good surface, though watch out for the ruts. The reservoir of Craig Goch comes into sight ahead, as you follow the track downhill to the left towards the road. Unfortunately this is not a pleasant descent, as the ruts force you to ride on a narrow strip on the outside of the hill with a steep drop uncomfortably close to your wheels.

7. From here the on-road section back to the

start proved very pleasant on a mid-week day in winter, with plenty of fast downhills, great views, and not a single car all the way. Turn right, passing the farmstead at Hirnant and bearing left past Esgair Cris after a good downhill. This brings you to the dam at the head of Penygarreg reservoir, which is a magnificent sight with tons of water cascading down its front. If you want to stop here, there is a beautifully sited picnic table on the other side.

8. The road continues from the bridge crossing the reservoirs beneath Graig Dolfaenog, with a fair amount of up and down as you ride back to the car park above Elan Village. The village itself is no more than a few houses with neither pub or shops, though the architecture is attractive. From there you can follow the valley bottom road back towards Rhayader; alternatively there are a number of offroad options available, such as taking the track that leads up past Carn Gafallt to get a view from the other side.

> ### Places To Visit:
> Elan Village and Information Centre; Rhayader also has an Information Centre.
>
> ### Pubs and Cafés:
> A choice of pubs and cafés in Rhayader.

5 Radnor Forest Circuit

Offroad and On-Road

Area: Powys – a tour of the Radnor forest. Start and finish at New Radnor, just off the A44. Roadside parking.

OS Map: Landranger 148 – Presteigne & Hay-on-Wye area.

Route:
New Radnor (GR:213610)
Whinyard Rocks (GR:210629)
Ednol Hill/Radnor forest (GR:228642)
Pentre (GR:240665)
Bleddfa/A488 (GR:207683)
Fishpools/A488 (GR:191683)
Graig (GR:173673)
Bridleway/road junction south of
Llanfihangel Rhydithon (GR:154662)
Water-break-its-neck waterfall
(GR:185602)
A44 (GR:194593)
New Radnor (GR:213610)

Nearest BR Station: Dolau, about a mile (1.5km) from Llanfihangel Rhydithon on north-west corner of circuit.

Nearest Youth Hostel: Glascwm, accessible by the A44/A481 and bridleway to the south of the route at GR:158532.

Approx Length: 21 miles (34km).

Time: Allow 4 hours.

Rating: Moderate. It is a fairly strenuous ride; some of the tracks can be extremely muddy; there are plenty of ups and downs.

This ride takes you on a tour of the Radnor Forest area of mid Wales, where a big area of hills and forestry is bounded by the A44 in the south and the A488 in the north. There are some steep climbs, but most of the climbing is on metalled tracks and lanes, and the ride ends with a great crossing of the wild moor to the west of Radnor Forest, culminating in a magnificent downhill section beneath the peak of Nyth-grug.

1. Park in New Radnor, just off the A44. There is plenty of on-road parking, and the village has two pubs, two well stocked general shops and a greengrocer. The ride starts fairly savagely with a long uphill. From the main street by the pub, turn right into Church Street and then after a short distance take a lane going left by a dead-end sign. Follow this uphill, ignoring signs to right and left for bridleways – it is a hard enough climb on tarmac.

2. Eventually you come to Forestry Commission territory ahead. The lane bears left round the side of the woods with a yellow footpath sign; you fork right onto the hard forestry track, following it as it snakes right, left and right again uphill through the woodland on a good surface that is easy climbing.

3. Eventually you reach the top and ride into open country on the north-east side of the woods by a large, modern barn close to Whinyard Rocks. Go through the gate, and follow the hard track ahead along the hillside with fine views out over the valley below.

4. Keep on this up and down track along the side of Bache Hill until you reach the next gate, which takes you into a rather depleted area of forestry at the top of Ednol Hill. Unlike much forestry, the tracks are easy to follow here. Bear right and follow a fast track downhill through the woodland, ignoring a right fork and going straight over a crossing track, and on down a narrower, steeper track with trees close on both sides until you come out at the edge of the forest. Go straight on through a rickety old gate

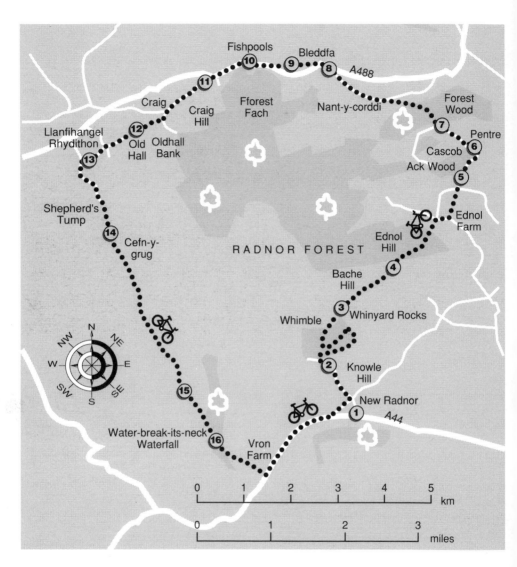

here, and down the right side of the field ahead – this is a bridleway, though completely unmarked. Ride on through a gate on the right, following the grass track down to the lane ahead. Turn right along this lane until you reach Ednol Farm.

5. A bridleway track turns left between the farm buildings, taking you across fields towards Ack Wood. At the edge of the woods go straight over a crossing track, and on down the right side of the woods on a medium fast grassy descent until you reach the next gate. Go through here, down a well overgrown track until you emerge by the side of a small, pink house.

6. You join a lane here, carrying straight on downhill to come to the hamlet of Pentre by the

A steady climb brings you to the top of the hill by Whinyard Rocks from where things get better and better.

bridge that crosses the stream. Turn left here, taking the next right fork by a dead-end sign before you reach the telephone box. This is another steep uphill on tarmac; when the hill begins to level out you take the first right turning signposted to Wood Farm.

7. When you reach the farmstead, go straight ahead through a gate into more forestry, bearing left and riding downhill across a wide crossing track. When we rode it this part of the downhill trail was covered by chopped down bits of trees, making the going tricky. Carry on downhill in the same direction past the next crossing track, which is as flat and wide as a motorway.

Farther down, the track can be extremely muddy as it levels out past the gate that takes you out of the forestry area. When you see the farmhouse at Nant-y-corddi, a modern building on the hillock to the left, go through the gate by the house and ford the stream to join a metalled lane for a short uphill on the other side.

8. This lane soon brings you to the A488, where you turn left and pedal a short way up the hill to the 100 Years pub. This is at the half-way point of the ride, just under two hours and 10 miles (16km) out from New Radnor. We passed by here too early to try the pub, but it looks a welcoming place with outside seating for muddy bikers, and additional interest is provided by the art gallery opposite.

9. To continue from Bleddfa you go west, either on-road or offroad. If you have plenty of energy, the offroad route follows a lane that forks off to the right, marked by a dead-end sign about 50 yards past the pub. This takes you uphill on a tarmac surface, and then along a grassy track on the hillside with several gates on the way, before rejoining the A488 at Fishpools after just short of a mile.

10. Keep straight on along the A44, which as A roads go is reasonably quiet and pleasant enough riding. Ignore the first track, which turns off uphill to the left, and after a mile or so take the second track, which goes straight ahead downhill to the left, as the road bends right by a right-hand fork.

11. Follow this track straight along – it is fast riding – passing an old black painted railway wagon in an unlikely position. Ride on past the track going up to the left opposite a couple of houses well hidden by trees, and follow the main track downhill towards Graig, taking the next sharp left turn onto a rough track that leads to a gate some 50 yards uphill – do not overshoot to where the track joins a lane that leads back to the A488.

12. Go through the gate here, following the track on an easy uphill as it bears round to the left with forestry on the hillside ahead. A track bears off to the right well before the woods; follow this downhill to the gate in the corner of a field, and ride on past a large barn opposite more woods. The track is deeply rutted and the going can be very muddy here, as it leads downhill to the picturesque farmstead at Old Hall, passing a stone wall with the main farm buildings over to the right. Ride straight on past the small duck pond on the left, and up through a gate. Follow the track until it bears right through another gate at the top of a field; go through, ignoring the turning immediately to the left, and after about 50 yards turn left uphill through a third gate well before you come to the large house ahead.

13. Follow this grassy track uphill by the side of a hedge, keeping on past a modern barn and joining a tarmac lane over a cattle grid. This leads to a crossroads above Llanfihangel Rhydithon – the nearest point on the route to a railway station – where you turn left on tarmac for the last significant climb of this ride. Follow the lane on a steady uphill until you come to a barn at Shepherd's Tump by sheep pens on the top of the ridge. Here you carry straight on ahead through a gate, joining a grassy track over good ground heading in a south-south-east direction.

14. From here on it is brilliant riding in a fine wilderness area to the west of Radnor forest, with good tracks leading along the tops of the hills and spectacular views if the weather is clear. Navigation is fairly straightforward, though every now and then you will need to check the compass and map. Past the ridge of Cefn-y-grug ignore the fork going left steeply uphill, and follow the track ahead as it bears right round the side of a great natural bowl carved into the landscape – we had time to admire the view as we had a puncture here – before keeping on ahead by the side of a fence on a great long downhill.

15. The track dips down into a gully to cross the Mithil brook where you head up the other side, taking the left track, which soon turns into another downhill. Keep on in the same direction beneath Nyth-grug, and you soon come to a hard track that gives a brilliantly fast downhill as it bears left round the hillside. Go through the gate by the modern barn, and continue down the track through the forestry. Take care as my companion rider was unseated here and had a hard landing; he was unhurt as he was dressed for winter riding, but in summer it could have been a different story.

16. From here you can divert to visit the extraordinarily-named Water-break-its-neck waterfall, which is on the east side of the Warren Plantation woodland. To get there you have to double back on a track joining the main track from the left; it is easy to miss if you are haring down at speed, and if you find yourself level with Vron Farm over to the left you have overshot it. Both tracks lead on down to the A44, where you turn left for a final five fast minutes of pedalling back to New Radnor.

Places To Visit:
Water-break-its-neck waterfall.

Pubs and Cafés:
Pubs at New Radnor and Bleddfa.

6 Powys Hills Circuit

**Offroad and
On-Road**

Area: Powys – a tour of the border country including the Hergest Ridge. Start and finish at the Information Centre at Kington on the A44 west of Leominster.

OS Map: Landranger 148 – Presteigne & Hay-on-Wye area.

Route:
Kington (GR:291567)
Hergest Ridge (GR:255564)
Gladestry/B4594 (GR:231551)
Colva (GR200531)
Glascwm (GR:158532)
Doctor's Pool (GR:155507)
Painscastle (GR:167463)
Glasnant (GR:185508)
Dreavour Farm (GR:186523)
Colva (GR200531)
Gladestry/B4594 (GR:231551)
Upper Hergest (GR:265550)
Kington (GR:291567)

Nearest BR Station:
None within easy reach.

Nearest Youth Hostel: Glascwm at GR:158532.

Approx Length: 28 miles (45km).

Time: Allow 5 hours.

Rating: Moderate. Very good riding, but care needs to be taken with navigation. Plenty of climbs, but nothing too hard.

While riding in the Brecon Beacons it is worth exploring the Welsh hills to the north, particularly those at the eastern end bounded by the English towns of Kington and Hay-on-Wye. They are much more forgiving than the Beacons to ride, with excellent tracks and narrow lanes criss-crossing the moorland countryside and joining the various hill ranges in this very quiet part of Britain. This route gives some excellent hill riding, together with a panoramic trip along the Hergest Ridge on the way to and from Kington. It can be adapted and modified to suit your time and inclinations; there are a huge number of other tracks and trails in the area waiting to be discovered.

1. Start from Kington, a pleasant small town on the border between England and Wales. From the Information Centre head west, turning right by the church and then left uphill towards Hergest Croft Gardens (world famous and open to the public in season) on a narrow, dead-end lane that takes you steadily and quite steeply straight uphill for around three-quarters of a mile (1km). When you come to a gate with open country beyond, go through and follow the wide grassy track ahead. This is the Hergest Ridge ride, one of the few bridleway sections of the Offa's Dyke long distance footpath that divides England from Wales.

2. The climb from here is easy, and you are soon on level ground along the grass track on top of the ridge with splendid views on all sides. Ignore all other tracks, and follow the main track as it bears round to the left, passing an incongruous mini plantation of monkey puzzle trees and a small pool near the top of the ridge at 1,390ft (423m). From here you pick up occasional long distance footpath markers, forking left and passing another lonely pool to the right. You then start a steep downhill on the grassy track, heading towards a prominent knoll.

3. The track bears left round the side of the knoll, joining a rough stone surface that soon leads downhill to the outskirts of Gladestry.

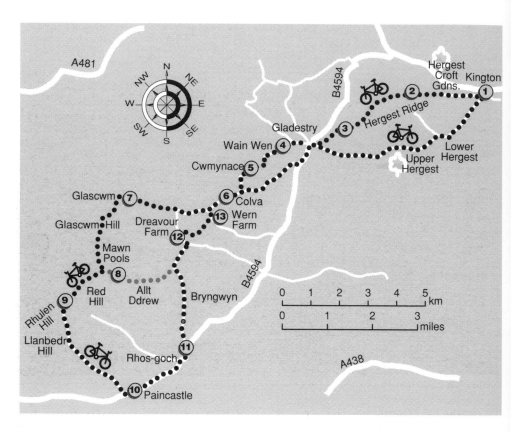

Bear right on the lane by the Offa's Dyke sign, and then take the first left past the pub. We found this a pleasant, welcoming place with outside seating, but since this stage is fairly early in the ride it may be better to postpone a visit until the return section. Take the right turn past the church, and then turn left again up the side with a barn on the right.

4. Take the next left fork and follow the narrow lane ahead, turning right at a T-junction. Some way on you come to the farmstead at Wain Wen. Here the tarmac lane comes to an end and bridleway takes over, but there is no signposting and the way is none too obvious. Bear left and right through the farmyard past the back of the house, turning left uphill through a gate and riding on up the side of a field by a fence, following the track round to the

right along the side of a forestry plantation at the top of the hill. At the next gate the track ahead becomes less distinct, apparently bearing north to head up into the high hills ahead.

5. This is not the way to go. Bear left onto a less distinct track, which takes you to the gate ahead on the far side of the field, leading on down past the old longhouse style farm and byre at Cymynace. Here it becomes a tarmac track, going through the gate at the bottom of the valley beneath the house before you ride steeply uphill on the other side and follow the track to the road by Llanhaylow farmhouse.

6. Turn left along this quiet, pleasant road, riding past the church at Colva, ignoring the first left turning, and following the road steeply downhill to cross the River Arrow at the next

So many places to stop and soak up the countryside when riding in this magic corner of Britain.

crossroads. Go straight over here, heading towards Glascwm. At the top of the hill, before you drop down into Glascwm (where there is a Youth Hostel), there is a track heading straight up the hillside above where you come to open land, by the side of a hedged field. Head up this track, which is steep, but not too steep to ride, and navigate your way to the big Mawn Pools to the south, which are found on the highest land on these hills.

7. Once it has gained some height the track passes through heather and is good riding, though care needs to be taken with direction and a compass is necessary. Take the first turning to follow the track along the hillside and then turn off to the north to continue climbing, gradually coming over the top with the Mawn Pools on your left. As you start to go down the other side take the left fork, which is a more rocky track, bearing round to the right and gradually dropping downhill to a small pool where the track crosses the bridleway coming up from Rhulen.

8. If you prefer to cut across country direct to Glasnant on a purely offroad route, turn left along the bridleway by the Doctor's Pool, following it eastwards over level ground to Allt Dderw. This is good fast going with some minor ups and downs in wild surroundings, and there are fine views over the valley to the right. As the track gets closer to the road it begins to bear left, before dropping down a steep, stony track on a hillside to join a tarmac lane on a hairpin bend. Take the left lane here, going through the gate that tells you it is for Glasnant Farm only – it is a bridleway, so do not worry. The tarmac soon disappears, as the track drops on a gentle downhill, passing the drive to the farmhouse and crossing a stream. From here it heads back uphill, before going steeply down to the road close by a farm – when I rode by it was notable for some ferociously yapping dogs. Turn left along the road here, and then left again along the side of the valley following the sign for Glascwm.

9. Alternatively, if you prefer to ride on via Painscastle using mainly very minor country roads, follow the track ahead from Doctor's Pool along the side of Red Hill, with the hillside falling steeply down to the Rhulen valley on the right below. This is a good riding on a fast surface, following the side of a wall and fence. After an easy up and down over a hillock the track hits the road on a bend at the top of Rhulen Hill, where you turn left and follow the road downhill all the way into Painscastle. It is fast going all the way down from Llanbedr Hill and you are unlikely to meet many cars, but watch out for the sheep that wander across the road on the grass and bracken moorland.

10. Painscastle, about 6 miles (10km) northwest of Hay-on-Wye, is a small hamlet with a friendly pub that is used to catering to horse riders who are hill trekking in the region. It is an optional place to start this ride from, though apart from the pub there is no obvious place to park. Before leaving Painscastle you may also like to extend the route into the small area of hill and moor to the south known as The Begwns – there is an excellent track that runs from east to west across them, and you could put together a quick tour of the area in less than an hour.

11. Painscastle is about the half-way point in the ride, with all kinds of options for getting back to Kington. The easiest route is totally on-road, following the B4594 direct to Gladestry. A more interesting alternative route turns off the B4594 at Rhos-goch to follow an up and down lane northwards across hill and moor via Bryngwyn to Glasnant.

12. When you come to the large buildings of Dreavour Farm, there is a bridleway track that snakes round the south side of the hill called Yr Allt. There is no sign for the bridleway but the farmer confirmed its existence; turn right into the farmyard, head towards the farmhouse, and then bear left and right between farm buildings. You have to hop off to cross a stream, and then you join a good track that climbs steadily round the side of the hillside, passing a small ruination of abandoned cars and a tiny but very beautiful ancient barn on the way. At the road, turn left steeply uphill, passing Wern Farm and rejoining the outward route on the road to Gladestry by turning right at the next crossroads.

13. From here it is mainly a fast and very pleasant on-road downhill into Gladestry. To get back to Kington you can either head back along the Hergest Ridge, starting with a savage climb but once on top enjoying a lovely ride down towards Kington. Alternatively, if you prefer to stay on-road follow the minor road past the Offa's Dyke sign, keeping left for the hamlets of Upper Hergest and Lower Hergest as you follow the bottom of the ridge above the River Arrow for a pleasant 5 miles (8km) or so back into Kington.

Places To Visit:
Hergest Croft Gardens near Kington.

Pubs and Cafés:
Pubs and cafés at Kington;
pubs along the route at Gladestry and Painscastle.

7 Offa's Dyke

Offroad and On-Road

Area: Powys and Shropshire. Start and finish at Knighton, west of Ludlow on the A4113. Plenty of parking available.

OS Map: Landranger 137 – Ludlow, Wenlock Edge & surrounding area.

Route:
Knighton (GR:290723)
Graig (GR:251755)
Offa's Dyke (GR:258780)
Newcastle (GR:246823)
Offa's Dyke (GR:258821)
Clun (GR:300805)
Skyborry Green (GR:265744)
Knighton (GR:290723)

Nearest BR Station: Knighton.

Nearest Youth Hostel: Clun Mill at GR:303812.

Approx Length: 22 miles (35km).

Time: Allow 3 to 4 hours, depending on visit to Clun.

Rating: Moderate. There are two good climbs onto Offa's Dyke, but the tracks are mainly good going – even in wet weather – and navigation is reasonably straightforward.

The Offa's Dyke Path is one of Britain's great long-distance walking routes, stretching the length of the Welsh–English border from north to south. It is famed for its up and downs and its rain, but sadly for mountain bikers most of it is footpath only, with a only a few short lengths of bridleway open to riders. This route gives an excellent taste of what it is like.

1. Knighton is a fine, small border town, and a perfect place to start a mountain bike ride. It has all the facilities you could require, including the luxury of a mainline railway station and a splendid playground (located by the Offa's Dyke Information Centre and Youth Hostel and useful if you have children with you). Find your way to the north side of the River Teme, and just past the railway station turn left (north-west) along the Skyborry road, which follows parallel to the river as it gains height on the hillside. This is one of those lovely, narrow, quiet country roads with fine views over the valley ahead and easy up and down riding; best of all it appears to be seldom used by cars.

2. Ignore the first turning uphill to the right, and just past 3 miles (5km) out of Knighton take the narrow lane that turns 90 degrees straight up the hill at Graig. This leads up to a gate by a farmstead, where the OS map shows the bridleway bearing right along the hillside to a solitary building, and then heading due north. In practice this does not happen. The first part of the track is delightful, but once you reach the tumble-down home (inhabited) ahead, there is no clear sign of where to go or what to do. I took the option of riding back to the farm and consulting the woman at the farm, who said I was welcome to ride through the yard to join the bridleway the other side. This is not marked as right of way – so be circumspect, behave well, shut all gates, and if possible do ask permission. Past the farmyard join the track bearing right, and keep straight on ahead to the north. The track here is excellent riding, slowly gaining height on a good surface up the hillside and soon bringing you to an isolated modern barn above Llandinshop. Take the right-hand

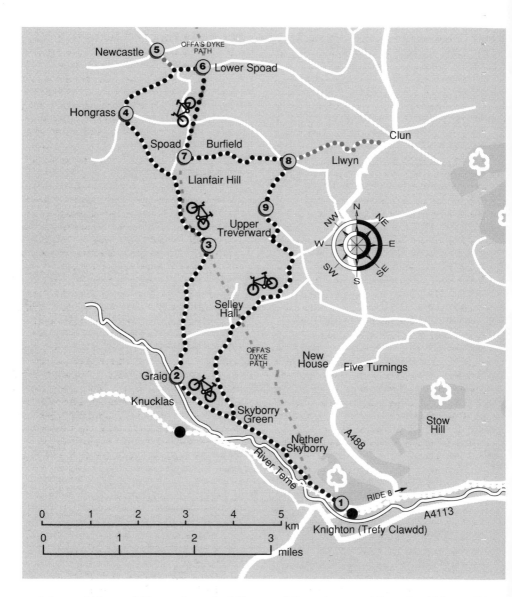

track here, which goes fairly steeply up the hill, but is still ridable to the top.

3. You cannot miss Offa's Dyke. It is an amazing structure running clearly along the ridge, which must have been built with considerable effort and precision. The long distance footpath follows the top – bikers should keep off here and indeed keep off the dyke altogether. Pause to take in the magnificent view across the valley of the River Teme before joining the hard track bridleway that follows the east side of the dyke going northwards.

4. Rain permitting this is great riding, passing a triangulation station at 1,410ft (430m) where the track crosses to the west side of the dyke, and then passing Llanfair Hill. Just past here I opted to leave the dyke, and keep with the main track bearing left to cross the lane ahead, bound for the hamlet of Newcastle at the bottom of the next valley. Go straight over the lane and onto a good track heading north-north-west on an easy uphill; at the top of the hill you come to a lane by Stoney Pound. Turn left and then almost immediately right by the side of a house here, following the narrow lane ahead all the way down to Newcastle. It is pretty steep, but not the sort of hill where you can really let rip – although there are unlikely to be cars, it is narrow, well strewn with mud and farm debris, and you cannot see round the corners! At the bottom turn left onto the B4368 Clun to Newcastle road, and ride across the bridge over the River Clun. The pub is a short distance on the right, and you will probably get to it in something less than two hours after leaving Knighton.

5. Having exhausted the delights of Newcastle (which also boasts a camp site), I opted to start the return circuit via some more of Offa's Dyke Path with a visit to the neighbouring village of Clun. Cross back over the River Clun, and ride along the B4368 eastwards. Ignore the first turnings going steeply right uphill, and after about half a mile (800m) look for the Offa's Dyke long distance footpath sign by the side of roadside farm buildings at Lower Spoad.

6. Go through the farmyard here, joining the track that goes steeply and if it is wet fairly muddily uphill, for what may be the first push of the ride. A short way up the hillside the track bears round to the left where the dyke reasserts itself; however you are on lumpy, bumpy ground with a fair incline, and riding is not easy. Never mind; as you gain height the views back across the valley of the River Clun are terrific, and near the top you hit a good track by the side of forestry, which soon brings you onto the ridge of Spoad Hill.

7. The OS map shows a bridleway bearing off to the south-east across the fields here, but it is not obvious on the ground and I opted to follow the route of the dyke and long distance footpath farther, turning right onto the lane by Springhill Farm and then left at the crossroads. The narrow lane bears left and dips to cross a small stream in the valley; as you start to head up look out for the offroad track that goes eastwards along the hillside, and follow this to the farmstead at Burfield.

8. From here on you are on tarmac, and it is fast riding to the crossroads ahead where you have the choice of turning right for the most direct country lane route back to Knighton, or going straight ahead to Clun. In its riverside setting with a castle, museum, pub and Youth Hostel this is a worthwhile diversion, and although the quickest way back to Knighton is then on the A road, it is more fun to backtrack along the route via Llwyn to the crossroads.

9. From here the lanes head southwards via Upper Treverward and Selley Hall, bound for Skyborry Green from where it is easy downhill all the way into Knighton. This is all on-road riding, but it is really pleasant with easy ups, good downs, and few if any cars in pleasant surroundings; if it is too tame there are at least a couple of offroad diversions that you can follow with time on your side and the OS map.

Places To Visit:
Offa's Dyke Information Centre in Knighton;
Clun offers a ruined castle (English Heritage – tel: 01345 056785), the Town Trust Museum and Clun Mill.

Pubs and Cafés:
A choice of pubs and cafés in Knighton; pub also at Clun.

8 Hopton Castle

Area: The Shropshire Hills to the west of Ludlow. Start and finish at Knighton, on the A4113 just inside Wales. Plenty of parking available.

OS Maps: Landranger 137 – Ludlow, Wenlock Edge & surrounding area.

Route:
Knighton (GR:290723)
Bedstone (GR:368758)
Hopton Castle (GR:367780)
Bedstone Hill (GR:346765)
Stow Hill (GR:310746)
Five Turnings (GR:287754)
Knighton (GR:290723)

Nearest BR Station: Knighton mainline station, or Hopton Heath just over 1 mile (1.5km) from Hopton Castle.

Youth Hostel: Knighton, temporarily closed at time of publication. Clun Mill at GR:303812 to the north of Knighton.

Approx Length: 20 miles (32km).

Time: Allow 3–4 hours.

Rating: Moderate. Some long climbs and navigation is not always straightforward; in wet weather you will find plenty of water on the top of Stow Hill.

This would make a good companion to the Offa's Dyke ride (Ride 7), making a full day out from Knighton or even a weekend's riding if you prefer to take things easy. As with so much of this area the riding can easily be extended both offroad and on-road, but some of the bridleways shown by the OS need to be taken with a pinch of salt, which may call for some creative route finding.

1. The route first goes to the north-east of Knighton, passing the railway station and following the A488 (very quiet for an A road, and when I last rode it flooded to a depth of a foot and a half!) for a mile or so to the turn-off for Weston. Follow the narrow lane here along the floor of the valley, keeping parallel with the railway line towards Bucknell. Half a mile or so past Weston you can follow a track along the hillside on the south side of Bucknell Wood, or stay with the road, which is the easy option. Both lead to Bucknell from where the B4367 heads north-east for Bedstone; if this seems too tame, follow the lane northwards up the hillside to Mynd, and from there round the edge of the forestry to Bedstone.

2. Turn up past the church at Bedstone – just a few houses and a massive college – following the very narrow lane between high hedges due north to Hopton Castle, a charming place with its own well preserved defensive keep. According to Forest News produced by Forest Enterprises, this is the official start of the Hopton Mountain Bike Trail. Instructions are vague – 'through Hopton Castle and turn left up track' – and when I rode up the track (which is bridleway) I found a locked gate to the forest. Never mind – the track on the other side bears left uphill and soon leads past mountain bike markers. With an eye on the map and a good sense of direction the fast forestry tracks can be followed round Hopton Titterhill to the top of Bedstone Hill, which is fast riding both up and down; you cannot imagine many walkers coming here, though do the right thing and hit the brakes to slow to their pace if you meet any.

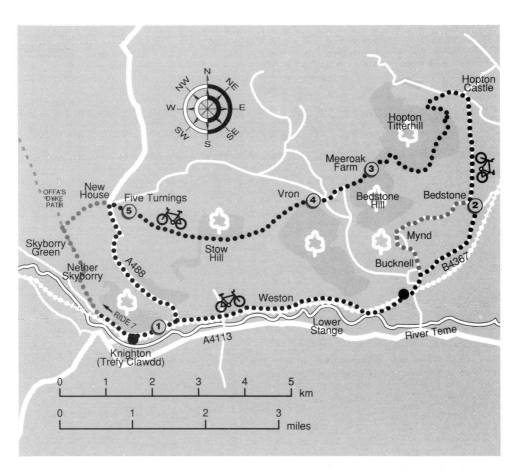

3. At the top of Bedstone Hill you come to a large Forestry Commission sign ('Caution! Mountain Bikes') by the driveway to Meeroak Farm. The OS map shows the bridleway going straight down the hill to the road here, but locked gates and stiles testified that it is not regularly used by horses even though it is passable by bike. If you do not like the look of this route, there is a pleasant track that heads south round the side of the forestry with great views out over the valley. I strayed onto it inadvertently but did not go all the way and therefore cannot vouch for it, but if you can find the way to Mynd and do not mind a diversion that adds some 4 miles (6km), it could well be a more satisfactory option, back-tracking west and north on-road.

4. The next bridleway turn-off leads westwards from the road along the north side of Bucknell Wood and up towards the farmstead at Vron; the metalled drive soon gives way to a rough track that is difficult riding up the side of the woods, and then it is a long, steady haul uphill on a good track past the high farm.

Half a mile (800m) or so on the bridleway track bears left to a gate where it joins a track emerging from Bucknell Wood, passing the hilltop triangulation station at 1,425ft (434m) and running level along the top of Stow Hill with woodland on the right. When I rode here it was extremely wet with the most incredible downpours of rain, but it remained ridable.

The Hopton Forest offers the chance of some fast riding on the way to a high point on Bedstone Hill.

5. Follow the track past the woodland, and then keep straight on along the side of fields until you hit a track that leads down to the road by a house at Five Turnings. From here the A488 leads down to Knighton and is the easiest way to go; I opted to push on west and follow the bridleway past New House, joining a section of Offa's Dyke Path, which is shown as bridleway by the OS Landranger as it heads southeast into Knighton. In practice this was not a success. Navigation was tricky and there was some severe cattle-churned mud on the way to the top of the hill; the views from here are magnificent, but the Offa's Dyke section appears to be only used as footpath, and ends with a desperately steep downhill by the side of Kinsley Wood that was really no fun on a bike at all!

Places To Visit:
Town Trust Museum at Clun;
Stokesay Castle (English Heritage – tel: (01588 672544) on the A49 north-west of Ludlow.

Pubs and Cafés:
Knighton has a choice of pubs and cafés.

9 Ludlow Forests

Offroad and On-Road

Area: Shropshire, west of Ludlow.

OS Map: Landranger 137 – Ludlow, Wenlock Edge & surrounding area.

Route:
Ludlow Castle (GR:506747)
Whitcliffe (GR:494741)
Mary Knoll Valley (GR:485733)
Bringewood (GR:460733)
Lady Halton (GR:478751)
Bromfield (GR:481769)
Priors Halton (GR:492752)
Ludlow Castle (GR:506747)

Nearest BR Station: Ludlow.

Nearest Youth Hostel: Ludlow at GR:513741.

Approx length: 13 miles (21km).

Time: Allow about 2 hours.

Rating: Easy. Be prepared for some straightforward hill climbing.

This is a short circuit in an area very close to Wales that is dominated by the defences of Ludlow's magnificent cliff-side castle. Much of the riding is in Mortimer Forest on the west side of Ludlow, with plenty of ups and downs on hard forest tracks followed by a leisurely tour of the massive, neighbouring Oakly Park estate before returning to Ludlow.

1. Ludlow Castle is very fine and well worth a visit, with its entrance on one side of the town square. If you are arriving by car, parking may not be so good, and I would recommend starting from the Whitcliffe Forest Office car park, which is sited 2 miles (3km) along the Wigmore road from Ludlow. From Ludlow Castle ride a short way into the town, and then head downhill through the old, narrow town gate (Ludlow was never designed for cars, which seem inappropriate and totally out of place), coming to traffic lights by the side of the River Teme. Cross the Ludford bridge to join the B4361, passing a church and the Youth Hostel on the left and turning off to the right just 100 yards or so uphill – the Whitcliffe Forest Office is signposted here.

2. Follow the road, which steadily gains height with a fine panorama opening out over Ludlow, and then keep on uphill past the start of Mortimer Forest on the left. It is a steady climb to the Whitcliffe Forest Office entrance where the wardens will no doubt be pleased to offer advice on various routes. Their policy on mountain biking is enlightened, and extends to all other forestry in the area with specific exclusions at Wyre: 'Our policy is to allow access to all woodland areas, but we do ask people to keep off the waymarked walking routes and to ride with consideration for others. The forest offers a haven of traffic-free roads and tracks for all the family to ride in a secure environment. Our Foresters and Rangers work hard to ensure that the small minority of cyclists who ride without thought for others are pressured to ride in a responsible manner.' In simple terms this means you can ride where you like, but keep off the specific walking routes and do not treat the

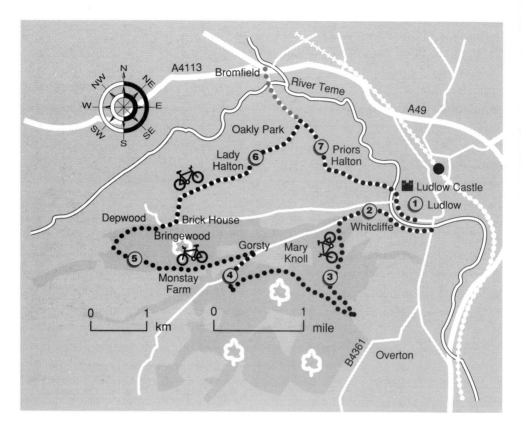

place as a race track. Take it easy, enjoy yourself, and when you come near to walkers, horse riders and any other forest users slow down to their pace.

3. The tracks and trails within the forest are easily followed, but as with all forestry it is easy to get lost and you need to keep a close eye on the map and your direction. I headed south on the main track and then picked up the track going north-west along the side of the Mary Knoll Valley, making for the High Vinnalls car park to connect with the road. If you are really enjoying the riding, you could easily double or treble the distance here by heading south into the Deer Park and Haye Park Wood areas.

4. At the High Vinnalls car park, join the road that is on the hillside above. Take care not to

stray into the special area for wheelchair users, which is right next door here – you will not be popular! Turn right along the road, heading steadily uphill to the next forestry turn-off at Gorsty, turning hairpin left to join a long, straight track that steadily gains height up the hillside. This is pleasant riding – and you are unlikely to meet many if any walkers – reaching a high point above Monstay Farm and then following the track downhill round the western end of the Bringewood forest.

5. Eventually the track leads down to an isolated old Water Board building, where you have the choice of following the main hard track, which hairpins its way round the hillside to the right, or plunging directly downhill on a straight track that gives a rough, bumpy ride to the bottom. Turn right to join the lane here, ignoring

Mortimer Forest is open to bikes and offers easy riding, but always be ready to give way to walkers.

the left turning to Deepwood and taking the next turning by the side of Brick House, the first building along this lane. This leads on a series of fast tracks – still fast but very muddy and wet if it has been raining – through the Lady Halton farmstead (bear left) and on to a junction with the main drive through Oakly Park.

6. You are now in the massive Oakly Park estate, owned and run by Lord Plymouth who lives in the mansion that can be glimpsed through the trees if you take the left turn along the drive towards Bromfield. This is a private road and bridleway, and it is worth the ride as far as the River Teme bridge, with a line of huge oaks leading down to the old, ruined water-mill with Bromfield Priory Gatehouse just beyond – this is a very fine building that has recently been renovated by the Landmark Trust. If by this stage you are desperate for a drink, the Clive Arms is on the other side of the busy A49 road (use the underpass); and from

here you could also link to the Wenlock Edge circuit (Ride 10) via Bromfield's race course.

7. To return to Ludlow follow the Oakly Park drive straight through the estate to the farmstead at Priors Halton. Here you join a narrow lane heading south-west towards Ludlow, and it is a great sight as you round a bend and once again see the castle on the cliff-side ahead. Ride across the bridge beneath it – this is unquestionably the best way to enter Ludlow – with a just a short uphill to the town square ahead of you.

Places To Visit:
Ludlow Castle and Buttercross
Museum.

Pubs and Cafés:
Ludlow has many pubs and cafés.

---

10 Long Mynd

Here is another mini classic, which takes you in a big circuit from the popular tourist town of Church Stretton along the magnificent Long Mynd ridge with only gliders for company. The route is approximately equally on-road and offroad, and apart from a very long uphill to the top of the Long Mynd is easily ridden most of the way.

1. Church Stretton, in the shadow of the huge Long Mynd ridge, is popular with tourists and easily reached by rail or car with the A49 main Shrewsbury road passing close by. The town has a large municipal car park that makes a good starting point, and its fair share of antique and tea shops, plus the handy Long Mynd Cycles if you need spares or feel the desperate urge to get a new bike. Turn left out of the car park into the main street, and then right along the B4370 towards Little Stretton. Thankfully the nearby A49 takes nearly all the traffic, as the B road wiggles through pleasant countryside and past small, elegant cottages on its way through Little Stretton.

2. From Little Stretton take the dead-end road uphill through Minton and on to Hamperley, passing through a farmyard and eventually leaving the road to follow a rough track along the side of fields. The bridleway continues south-west along the side of the woods at Churchmoor Rough, and for a short distance the way is none too obvious. Keep on ahead, and then on down by the side of a rough, bumpy field, bearing right down a lane by the farmstead beside the A489 at Horderley.

3. Turn right along the main road here. It follows the valley of the River Onny and would be much more pleasant if it was a country lane, but nevertheless it is not too bad. As the A489 goes downhill look out for the right turning at Plowden, going quite steeply uphill on the narrow road that leads north towards Asterton.

4. A few hundred yards up this hill the bridleway doubles back up the hillside on the right, passing through a gate. This is the start of a long, steady uphill to the top of the Long Mynd – the going is good, though steep, and the views over to Wales

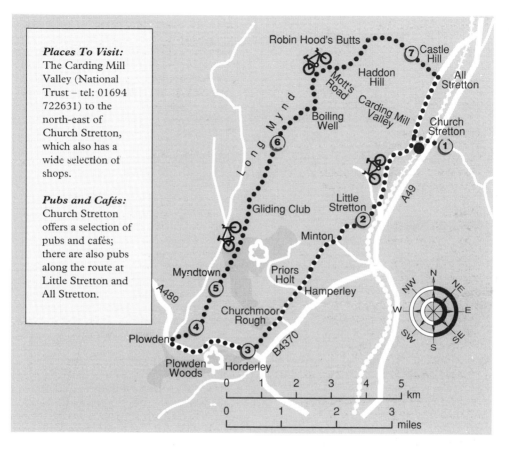

Places To Visit:
The Carding Mill Valley (National Trust – tel: 01694 722631) to the north-east of Church Stretton, which also has a wide selection of shops.

Pubs and Cafés:
Church Stretton offers a selection of pubs and cafés; there are also pubs along the route at Little Stretton and All Stretton.

get better as you go higher. Carry on through the sheep pens, bearing left with the main track to climb past Black Knoll.

5. Once on the top the track levels out into a series of gentle ups and downs, with extensive woodland on the right-hand (south-east) side of the ridge. Along the top of the ridge you approach the Long Mynd Gliding Club, with several signs warning you to keep to the trail. The club's driveway leads out onto the Portway, an ancient road that is now sadly a modern road and continues along the top of the ridge.

6. The Portway is nonetheless pleasant riding, and continues past the triangulation station at Pole Bank, the high point of the ride at 1,690ft

(516m). Just past here you can cut the ride short at Boiling Well by taking the right turn going steeply downhill into Church Stretton; better to turn left towards Ratlinghope for some more offroad (this road was closed to cars when I rode here) before turning off on the first bridleway track to the right. This leads across open moorland, bearing right downhill past Mott's Road – a direct bridleway route to Church Stretton via the Carding Mill Valley – and then swinging east at Robin Hood's Butts for a really good downhill across open grassland towards the valley below.

7. At Plush the track hits the road, which winds steeply on downhill into All Stretton. From there it is just over a mile along the B4370 back to Church Stretton.

11 Wenlock Edge

Offroad and On-Road

Area: Shropshire, following the Wenlock Edge ridge between Aston Munslow and Much Wenlock.

OS Map: Landranger 137 – Ludlow, Wenlock Edge & surrounding area. Landranger 138 – Kidderminster & Wyre Forest area.

Route:
Aston Munslow (GR:512867)
Little London (GR:505884)
Stanway Manor (GR:525915)
Wilderhope Manor (GR:546929)
Hilltop (GR:570963)
Much Wenlock (GR:624000)
Shipton (GR:563920)
Aston Munslow (GR:512867)

Nearest BR Stations:
Craven Arms, Church Stretton.

Nearest Youth Hostel: Wilderhope Manor at GR:544928.

Approx Length: 22 miles (35km).

Time: Allow 3 to 4 hours, possibly longer in wet weather.

Rating: Moderate. No hard riding, but some of the tracks can be gruesomely muddy if it has been wet; serious horse country!

Wenlock Edge is a place with a great reputation – it also has a bridleway for much of the way along its length, which makes it a good place for a ride. There are plenty of attractions along the route including the famous Wenlock Priory, and it could also make a good companion to the nearby Ludlow Forests (Ride 9) and The Long Mynd (Ride 10) routes.

Wenlock Edge was celebrated by the poet A. E. Housman:

> *On Wenlock Edge the wood's in trouble;*
> *His forest fleece the Wrekin heaves;*
> *The gale, it plies the saplings double,*
> *And thick on Severn snow the leaves.*

That was written in the last decade of the nineteenth century, and I do not think Housman would find too many changes on Wenlock Edge today. Cars and road building have obviously left their unpleasant mark, but compared to much of Britain this particular area has come off relatively unscathed.

This ride is road one way, bridleway and a short length of road the other. I opted to start from Aston Munslow where there is a small car park conveniently opposite the pub; this enables you to tackle the offroad section first, get to Much Wenlock in time for lunch and a stroll round Wenlock Priory, and leave the long road section until last. If you do not mind a bit of distance it also makes a useful connection with the Ludlow Forests ride, with about 9 miles (14km) of pleasant pedalling on level country roads between Aston Munslow and Bromfield – via Corfton, Culmington and Ludlow Race Course.

1. At Aston Munslow follow the narrow lane uphill by the side of the pub, forking right to pass the White House – this is a private museum of farm relics, now owned by the Landmark Trust and only open to the public by prior appointment. Farther up the hill bear right at a T-junction, following the bridleway sign and looking for a track turning uphill to the left in an area where there is more than likely to be plenty of horse action.

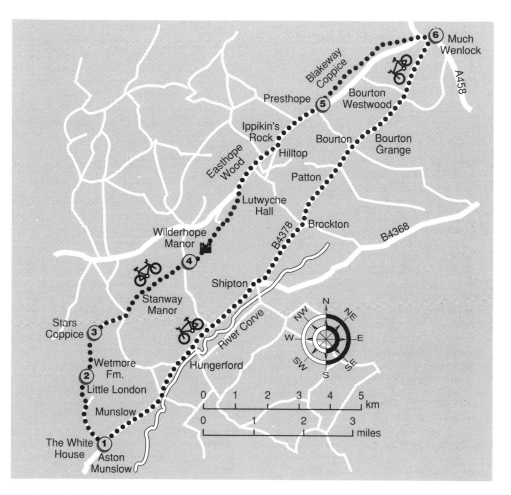

2. The track that follows is the first true offroad section of the ride, and if it has been wet it can be gloriously muddy. It bears left through the trees on the ridge ahead, passing the triangulation station at 1,060ft (323m) and then heading down the hillside towards Wetmore Farm. Maybe this is always a wet area, for the track down the hill can get like a horse-churned quagmire, and once you are past the farm – an odd, shambolic sort of place – the wide track that goes ahead through the woods can be even worse!

3. Follow the track past Star Coppice, bearing north-east and keeping in that direction all the way

to Much Wenlock. The track levels out and gets better, joining the road for 50 yards or so by Roman Bank before joining another track that continues to follow Wenlock Edge. Cross straight over at the next lane, joining the metalled track that leads to Wilderhope Manor; just before you reach it, watch out for the horse made of old horseshoes! Wilderhope Manor looks a gloomy kind of place. It is run as a no-smoking Youth Hostel and is owned by the National Trust ,who open it to the general public on Wednesday and Saturday afternoons from April to September.

4. A good, fast track leads on from Wil-

En route to Wenlock there is good signposting to help point the way through the hillside woodland.

derhope Manor, passing the much smarter and privately owned Lutwyche Hall a little farther on, and then joining with the B4371 road besides Easthope Wood. Sadly and unforgivably there is no bridleway along Wenlock Edge here, so you will need to pedal on the road, passing the pub at Hilltop before coming to Knowle Quarry – owned by the National Trust and open to the public with a 'quarry walk' round the old kilns, quarry works, stables and tramway that were last in use in 1925.

5. Here the unsignposted bridleway turns sharp left off the road, joining an excellent track, which passes below the quarry and bears north-east along the hillside. The surface is hard with gentle ups and downs as you head through a dense woodland of ash, wych-elm, oak, silver birch and crab apple in the Blakeway Coppice – these are very pretty trees but they do block the view! Where the track forks left and right just past a bench with a local horse trail sign, take the right fork uphill. This leads into open country at the edge of National Trust land, joining a hard track that soon heads quickly downhill into Much Wenlock to join the road on the outskirts of this Shropshire market town. It is best known for the romantic ruins of Wenlock Priory, set amidst fine lawns and ornamental topiary, and administered by English Heritage.

6. If Aston Munslow was your starting point it is

a steady plod of around 12 miles (20km) to return along the B4378. Road-haters may prefer to retrace their tracks along the outward offroad route. The road is hardly classic riding, but the countryside is pleasant, the cars are not too bothersome, and there are no serious hills along the way. At about the half-way point the privately owned Shipton Hall is sometimes open to the public and will serve an afternoon tea, perhaps getting you back to Aston Munslow in time for a much needed thirst-quencher at the pub.

Places To Visit:
Wenlock Priory (English Heritage – tel: 01345 056785) and Guildhall;
Wilderhope Manor (National Trust – tel: 01694 771363);
Shipton Hall;
The White House Museum;
Stokesay Castle (English Heritage – tel: 01345 056785).

Pubs and Cafés:
There are plenty of pubs and cafés in Much Wenlock;
pubs can also be found along the route at Brockton, Aston Munslow and Hilltop.

12 Kerry Ridgeway

Offroad and On-Road

Area: Powys and Shropshire, following the old Kerry Ridgeway ridge route between Bishop's Castle and the A483 near Gwynant. Start and finish at Bishop's Castle, just off the A488 north of Clun

OS Map: Landranger 137 – Ludlow, Wenlock Edge & surrounding area. Landranger 136 – Newtown, Llanidloes & surrounding area.

Route:
Bishop's Castle (GR:323885)
Churchtown (GR:263473)
Clun forest (GR:225860)
Felindre (GR:168813)
Cider House (GR:110847)
Kerry Ridgeway (GR:150863)
Bishop's Castle (GR:323885)

Nearest BR Station:
Newtown and Craven Arms.

Nearest Youth Hostel: Clun Mill, south of Bishop's Castle at GR:303812.

Approx Length: 30 miles (48km).

Time: Allow 4–5 hours.

Rating: Moderate. It is a fair distance with a few good hills (mainly on-road); no great problems with mud or horses in wet weather.

This is a wonderful ride along the Welsh–English border, making the most of the Kerry Ridgeway, an old drove road that once connected Bishop's Castle with farmsteads to the west. Most of the offroad is easy and very enjoyable; the on-road part is probably more demanding with some keen hills, passing through great countryside with few cars to bother you. All you need is the weather – this can be an exposed ride and is best left for a fine day!

1. Bishop's Castle is a very attractive small town, named after its ancient motte and bailey that no doubt played its part in the days when the English were at war with the Welsh. Allow time for a look round, and then find your way to the big church at the bottom of the main street on the southern extremity of the town. Turn right here, and then follow the lane uphill, taking a left turn at the first crossroads. At first this leads you through a modern housing estate, then onto a dead-end road that gets narrower and rougher as it bears left and right past a farmstead. It leads up to another farm on the hillside by the start of extensive woodland; keep straight on here, going through a gate and joining a rough track that heads up the side of the woods before breaking into open country farther up the hill.

2. The views from here back over Bishop's Castle are pretty good, as you plod on up the side of a field, bearing left and right to reach the top of Colebatch Hill (the bridleway is not too obvious), keeping on the left side of the fence and riding across grass towards a farm building to join the lane ahead. Turn left here, and then after about 50 yards turn right up a straight grass track, following it between stunted trees by the side of Reilth Top, and then joining a track that heads downhill past an isolated barn, bearing left and going steeply down the hillside towards Reilth Farm – all this takes place in impressive country! Just before the farm, follow the sign to the right and go down to the road, turning right along the bottom of the valley, and then second left for Churchtown.

3. Past the pretty Churchtown church, which stands on its own in the valley, you cross the

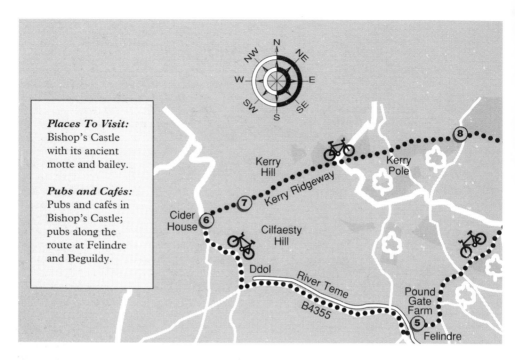

Places To Visit:
Bishop's Castle with its ancient motte and bailey.

Pubs and Cafés:
Pubs and cafés in Bishop's Castle; pubs along the route at Felindre and Beguildy.

Offa's Dyke Path and then hit Churchtown Hill; from there it is a long plod to the top at Two Crosses. Go straight ahead at the five-way cross-roads here, starting on a hill that heads down the side of the woodland and then goes steeply down the Cwm Moch valley in Clun forest, bearing right by Brook House and then going straight ahead onto a metalled farm track at the next T-junction.

4. This leads you down to Curney Farm where the way is not too obvious; just turn 90 degrees right along the edge of the fields, going through the gate ahead and heading down the exposed hill-side as you ride onto OS Landranger 136. You will soon find the track, which brings you steeply down to the road at an isolated crossroads. Go straight ahead here (south-west) for a long, steady uphill between Kents Bank and Black Mountain, keeping south-west past Corkins Bank and Pound Gate Farm, with a high-speed downhill to the B4355 Knighton road at Felindre. There is a pub here; it was not open when I passed, and the one down the road at Beguildy (Knighton direction) looked rather more jolly.

5. From Felindre it is 7 miles (11km) or so on-road to the start of the Kerry Ridgeway at Cider House. It is pleasant enough riding, and you know you are getting there when the road starts to zigzag up the hillside, breaking into open moorland as it passes the border sign on the exposed hilltop. Cross the cattle grid and then start to freewheel down the other side, looking for the farmstead of Cider House, which is about half a mile (800m) on. When I passed by it appeared to have been unoccupied for some years – nevertheless it is in a fine position on a wild hillside with a coppice of trees to protect it.

6. Immediately opposite, a track turns off to the right along the ridge of the hill. This is the Kerry Ridgeway, and though not signposted, it is a bridleway. With a few road sections and hard forestry tracks it will take you along the top of the ridge for 17 miles (27km) or so, all the way to Bishop's Castle. It starts on a good track, heading dead straight on a slight uphill, before crossing empty fields with wild moors to the south and fine views over the Newton Valley to the north.

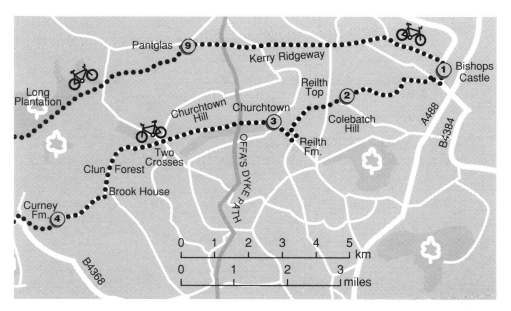

7. Navigation is pretty simple; you just keep straight on, passing an isolated pond by 'Two Tumps', and then joining a fast track by the forestry on Kerry Hill that leads quickly on past Radnorshire Gate to the B4368. Keep straight on here past Block Wood, crossing a rough, bumpy field to the solitary house at Kerry Pole, and then following the road straight ahead. It is about 2 miles (3km) on tarmac here, and is not much used – all I encountered was a solitary, ancient Land Rover driven by a solitary, ancient shepherd.

8. At the next junction you are back onto forest tracks, passing extensive woodland on the left by Upper Short Ditch. Where the track forks, take the more obvious right fork, reaching a conveniently sited picnic bench up on the hillside, which is a good place to check the map as you ride back onto OS Landranger 137. Passing Long Plantation the track becomes forest road, and it is easy to turn off the Ridgeway inadvertently. The road bears right to follow the right side of a belt of trees near the end of the forestry, and this appears to be the way to go; in fact it soon turns south away from the Ridgeway, bringing you down past Mason's Bank to Two Crosses that you passed on the outward route. Instead look for the insignifi-

Time to stop for a map check or a bite to eat when you come to this lonely picnic table on the long ride from Cider House to Bishops Castle.

cant, unsignposted, overgrown track that goes straight ahead along the left side of the trees; ride along here to stay on the Ridgeway, joining a track at the end of the woodland where the Ridgeway changes as it winds along an old bumpy road before converging with the road proper at Pantglas.

9. From here it is about 6 miles (10km) straight along the top to Bishop's Castle. There should be few cars and you lose height almost all the way, which makes it fast, exhilarating riding due east, with a final extra-steep descent into the town at the end of this great ride.

13 Lan Fawr Ridge Ride

Offroad and On-Road

Area: Powys. From Montgomery via Lan Fawr and Chirbury to Montgomery. Start and finish at Montgomery on the B4388 south of Welshpool. Parking in and around the town.

OS Map: Landranger 137 – Ludlow, Wenlock Edge & surrounding area. Landranger 126 – Shrewsbury & surrounding area.

Route:
Montgomery (GR:221966)
Whitley (GR:246961)
Lower Lane (GR:260972)
Alport/A490 (GR:273953)
Old Church Stoke (GR:288952)
The Marsh (GR:302977)
Bromlow (GR:320019)
Rorrington (GR:301007)
Weston House Farm (GR:293985)
Chirbury (262983)
Montgomery (GR:221966)

Nearest BR Station:
Welshpool or Newtown.

Nearest Youth Hostel:
Clun Mill at GR:303812.

Approx Length: 21 miles (34km).

Time: Allow around 4 hours.

Rating: Moderate. Good riding, but be prepared to take care with the navigation. The steepest climbs are on-road.

This is a real little classic, starting in the wonderful small Welsh town of Montgomery, crossing Offa's Dyke Path through low country, and then climbing to follow the magnificent ridge of Lan Fawr with wonderful views over Wales to the left and England to the right. I rode it in foul weather with biting winds and heavy rain and enjoyed it; in fine weather it should be a great ride.

1. Montgomery is a delightful little place, a town that is no bigger than many villages. It is overlooked by a fine old castle on the hillside above, which is well worth climbing up to. The town square boasts a handful of shops, an interesting art gallery, and a tea shop, which was a great place to finish off the day. If you are into antiquities take time out to visit the church on the other side of the road, and see if you can locate the 'phantom' robber's grave. Turn right out of the main square, turning down the hill and out of town on the south bound B4385. Just before a right-hand bend look out for a bridleway track on the left, going through a gate in a fence and following the track along the side of the recreation ground. This leads to an ornamental park; turn right along a tarmac track between the two large ponds, and follow it between woods and out of the park until you reach a cattle grid by the crossing for the Offa's Dyke long distance footpath.

2. The OS map shows the bridleway turning right to follow the long distance footpath here, but it is a miserable way to go in wet weather, following the side of fields with no very obvious way out onto the road at Gwarthlow farm. It is better to go straight ahead along the tarmac lane to Whitley Farm – this is not shown as a right of way, but joins with a bridleway immediately behind the farmhouse.

3. Turn right through the gate, and cross the farmyard to the next gate, joining a track that follows the side of fields to the large farmstead at Timberth. Go straight ahead through the farmyard here, following a track downhill and then bearing left to follow the side of the woods

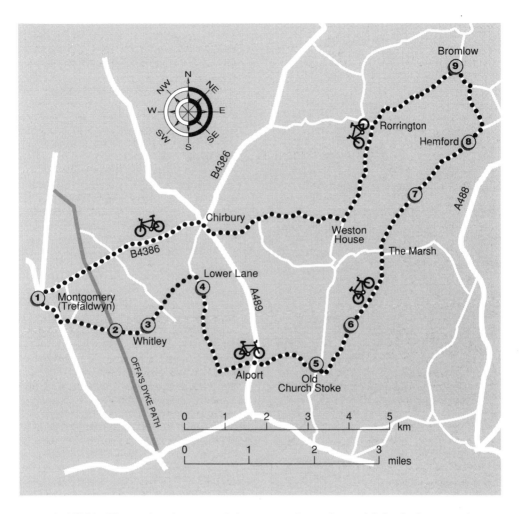

up on the hillside. The way here is not too obvious, but just keep going on across the next grassy field and you will come out onto Lower Lane, hopefully by the bridleway gate.

4. Turn right along the quiet country road here, taking a left turn at the T-junction at Rhiston. This soon leads across the main A490 at Alport; go down the steep hill ahead, joining a rough and sometimes muddy track to cross the river valley, and then steeply up the other side for a short way to come out on a smooth tarmac lane by Upper Brynkyn. This leads you

to the road; turn left by the house on the corner, and start to head uphill until you come to the pub at Old Church Stoke, which looks a welcoming place with fine views from the garden towards Montgomery and its castle.

5. Past the pub bear left and then sharp right by a telephone box, to head steeply up the side of the hill. As you approach the top look for an unmarked narrow tarmac lane on the left, which is the start of the ridge ride. Ride along this lane, which leads fairly steeply up between high hedges, eventually coming to a gate and joining

Bilingual rough-riders are particularly welcome when you head offroad in Montgomeryshire where Offa's Dyke still helps to keep the English out.

a rough track by the side of the solitary house in a magnificent position at Cowlton on the hilltop. From here there are tremendous views over the surrounding country, but it is also very open to the weather and I was forced to take refuge in a dilapidated barn while a good dose of Welsh rain lashed the hillside.

6. From here on the track is mainly good riding and easy to follow, keeping along the ridge past Lan Fawr and the forestry by Corndon Hill, before dropping downhill to cross the road above Priest Weston. On the other side the track becomes less distinct, bearing right by the

ancient Stone Circle at Mitchell's Fold and following a slight uphill to the top of Stapeley Hill with more superb views on all side.

7. When the track starts to go down the side of Stapeley Hill, take care with your navigation. It is a fast and enjoyable descent, and before you know it you will rush on down past the south side of the huge block of partly felled forestry ahead – this is the wrong way to go, and once at the bottom there is no easy way out from the area called Black Marsh. Slow down and look out for the correct bridleway route, which swings left to follow the top western side of the forestry, and then bears right down through the woods on a rough, bumpy track that can also be extremely muddy.

8. Beyond the forestry the route goes onto OS Landranger 126, joining a tarmac lane that leads to the road ahead above Hemford. Turn left at the crossroads here for the start of a long up and down section on very narrow country roads, many of which look almost forgotten as if they rarely ever see a car. A steep, winding descent leads into the valley, passing the pub above Bromlow, which appears to have been shut up for good.

9. Beyond Bromlow follow the signs to Rorrington with more ups and downs back onto OS map 137, then either going southwards straight ahead to the pub at Priest Weston below the Lan Fawr ridge, or turning right to Chirbury from where it is just over 2 miles (3km) along quiet roads back to Welshpool.

Places To Visit:
Montgomery has a fine ruined castle.

Pubs and Cafés:
Montgomery has a choice of pubs and a café. There are also pubs at Old Church Stoke, Priest Weston and Chirbury along the route.

---

14 Llanfair Caereinion Circuit

Offroad and On-Road

Area: Powys – a circuit to the south-west of Welshpool. Start and finish at Llanfair Caereinion, where there is a small, free car park up the hill going south on the B4389 towards Newtown.

OS Map: Landranger 125 – Bala and Lake Vyrnwy. Landranger 136 – Newtown, Llanidloes & surrounding area.

Route:
Llanfair Caereinion (GR:101064)
Bryn-penarth (GR:098047)
Llanllugan (GR:057023)
Mynydd Clogau (GR:043990)
Bwlch y Garreg (GR:012968)
Cefn Gwyn (GR:030006)
Llanllugan (GR:057023)
Tan-y-graig (GR:070035)
Llanfair Caereinion (GR:101064)

Nearest BR Station: Welshpool.

Nearest Youth Hostel:
None within easy reach.

Approx Length: 21 miles (34 km).

Time: Allow 4 hours.

Rating: Easy to moderate. Mainly easy riding with good tracks and straightforward navigation, though the narrow roads on the way out can be confusing.

The village of Llanfair Caereinion on the edge of the wild country of Powys is a pleasant enough little place to start this ride, on the main A458 west of Welshpool. Turn over the bridge that crosses the River Banwy, and then continue past the church to a small, signposted car park on the left. When you return there is a handy café here on the corner, as well as a choice of pubs and a fish and chip shop nearby.

1. Turn left out of the car park, heading up the hill. After a few hundred yards fork right off the B4389, following a minor road signposted to New Mills. Just a few yards on an unmarked track bears off to the left; this is the bridleway, a steady uphill on a good, hard surface. On the right it passes immaculate gardens at Bryn-glas with fields away to the left, snaking right and left more steeply uphill to join an old road that runs along the top of the hill between hedges – good going when it is dry but potentially quite muddy when it is wet.

2. Go straight ahead through the farmyard at Hengefn, opening and closing the gates as you go; the dog here was too sleepy to take much notice as I passed by. On the far side a hard track leads on uphill past hen coops, before heading down to join the road with a fine valley panorama ahead and the distant peaks of the hills of Mynydd Clogau ahead. There are all kinds of variations on the route to get to these hills, but I was pretty happy with the way I found, which mixed peaceful country lanes with an excellent offroad section.

3. When the farm track hits the road, turn left by the house on the corner and follow the road eastwards. The OS map shows a bridleway going due south downhill here, but it is by no means obvious, so ride on for about half a mile (800m) to the first right turning, which goes steeply downhill. Follow this narrow lane down into the valley. At the bottom the road bends left to cross a stream by a well hidden caravan park and camp site, and then bears right uphill. Where the road bends sharp left a track goes straight on along the side of the valley – this is the next bridleway section.

4. Follow the track past the farm on the right,

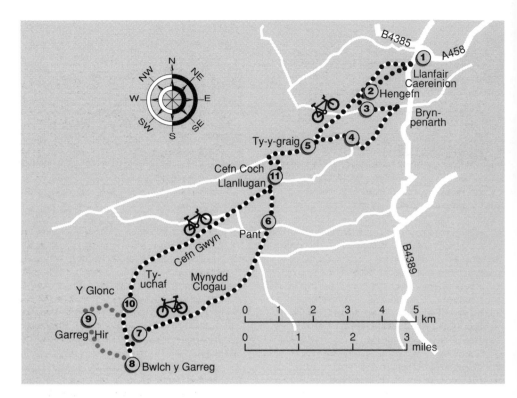

following an old road with a beautiful view over the valley and the Afon Rhiw below. Mostly the going is good, until you come to the final section of track, which follows an avenue of trees. When I rode it this part was impossibly muddy, with a mini torrent flowing down the middle after recent heavy rain; the answer is simply to go up the hillside a short distance, following hard ground above the track until you see the gate ahead and the road.

5. Turn west to follow the road towards Cefn Coch here, turning off after just under a mile to follow a narrow lane steeply downhill into the hamlet of Llanllugan. Follow the road straight through and uphill the other side, heading south over the crossroads to Pant. Less than half a mile farther on, just past a left turning, take the bridleway track that forks off to the right towards Mynydd Clogau, the start of a long offroad section.

6. From here on it is really good riding. The track is in excellent condition as it passes through a wild landscape on a steady uphill, bearing towards the south-west. It runs for just over 3 miles (5km) and is easy to follow to its south-western end where it starts to head downhill, passing a farmstead on the hillside below and to the right as Llyn Mawr comes into view. Here the track crosses a cattle grid to join a tarmac lane, with a number of options for the return route.

7. The simplest way is immediately to turn sharp right downhill along the driveway that goes towards the farmhouse. This joins the bridleway track passing the back of the farm buildings to head due north.

8. Another option is to find a pub – the nearest is at Pontdolgoch (GR:938012). Although a little way due south off the route it may provide an interesting diversion.

A track follows the hillside above the Afon Rhiw before the route breaks out into open country. Look out for the spectacular daffodils in early spring.

Game for a challenge? If you head out towards Garreg Hir there is some interesting unexplored country to the west, but it is not likely to be easy riding.

9. A third option is to seek out something a little more challenging. For some tastes the track across the moor may seem too easy, but if that is how you feel there are plenty of bridleway routes heading across more wild terrain with no such easy tracks to follow. The bridleway that runs along the south side of Llyn Mawr heads towards the highest point of the whole area, Garreg-hir at 1,590ft (485m). The turn-off is through a gate a short way down the lane for the farm, with a sign indicating that only cars with hang gliders are welcome. A good track leads on for a short way past Llyn Mawr, but from there you follow an indistinct track through the grass by the side of Garreg-hir in fine surroundings. The going is reasonable, though with bumps and lumps and a slight uphill some may prefer to walk it. From there on navigation gets a little tricky. After coming to high ground you cross what appears to be a really good track that is shown on the OS map reconnecting with the return trail. However something went wrong for me here and I ended up dragging the bike along a steep hillside through waist-high bracken, and then fording a deep stream cutting stuffed with the occasional dead sheep to find my way back to the trail. If you have got time to spare you could spend a pleasant few hours exploring the tracks and trails that go out towards Mynydd Dwyriw here; if not you would do better on the easy route.

10. Once back on the right track the going is straightforward, though the condition of this northbound track is poor in places with some enormous holes, which require slamming on the brakes and careful riding. Much too soon the offroad comes to an end, at the start of a long downhill passing a camp site and coming to crossroads at Glan-yr-afon. Once again there are all kinds of options for the return route from here. I chose to follow the river eastwards towards Llanllugan – this route passes a beautiful waterfall, and in the spring there is one long lane lined with daffodils from end to end.

11. Past Llanllugan rejoin the outward route for a while, following the road uphill and then bearing east and north-east towards Llanfair Caereinion – it is all agreeable and easy riding on very quiet roads. You can either ride on direct to the starting point from here, or at the top of the final downhill by the telephone box go a bit higher to rejoin the outward bridleway. This is the route I would recommend, finishing more offroad than on-road, with a good downhill back to Llanfair Caereinion

---

Places To Visit:
Welshpool & Llanfair Light Railway; Powis Castle (National Trust – tel: 01938 554336), south of Welshpool.

Pubs and Cafés:
Pubs and cafés in Llanfair Caereinion; pub at Carno.

North Wales

Wales is a hilly country, and there is nowhere more hilly than the north of Wales. Good offroad trails are not so easy to find here, but the eleven routes that follow cover the central part of this often wild and magnificent area. They make the most of old roads over the hills and forgotten country roads through the valleys to produce some truly memorable rides.

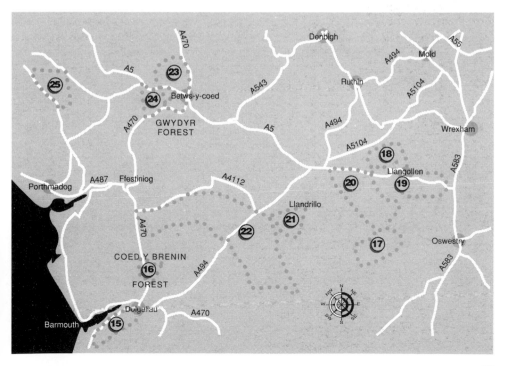

15 Beneath Cadair Idris

**Offroad and
On-Road**

Area: Gwynedd – a big circuit between Dolgellau and the coast in the shadow of Cadair Idris. Start and finish at Dolgellau.

OS Map: OS Map: Landranger 124 – Dolgellau.

Route:
Route:Dolgellau car park (GR:728179)
Llyn Gwernan (GR:705160)
Lynnau Cregennen (GR:663135)
Ffordd Ddu (GR:650127)
Rhydcriw (GR:633100)
Ffridd Bryn-coch (GR:620073)
Llanegryn (GR:601054)
A493/Rhoslefain (GR:577058)
Llwyngwril (GR:592095)
Morfa (GR:614111)
Cyfannedd (GR:634123)
Daran (GR:648138)
Arthog (GR:640148)
Old Penmaenpool–Morfa railway
(GR:660173)
Dolgellau car park (GR:728179)

Nearest BR Station:
Morfa Mawddach.

Nearest Youth Hostel: Kings Dolgellau at GR:683161.

Approx Length: 32 miles (51km); alternative Dolgellau and railway circuit 16 miles (26km), hill and coast circuit 22 miles (35km).

Time: Allow 5 hours for the full distance; 2 hours for the Dolgellau and railway circuit, 3 to 4 hours for the hill and coast circuit.

Rating: Moderate. The Dolgellau and railway circuit is fairly undemanding; the hill and coast circuit presents a tougher challenge.

This route makes a fine tour of the area of North Wales dominated by the magnificent mountain Cadair Idris. For those who prefer not to take on the challenge of the full distance in one go, it divides conveniently into two circuits, giving more time to take it easy and explore the area.

1. There is a large, convenient pay and display car park on the north side of Dolgellau, just by the bridge that crosses the Afon Wnion. This makes a good place to start this ride, and it is also well placed for exploring the small, interesting town on foot. An alternative starting point could be the car park at Morfa Mawddach station (GR:628142) by the mouth of the Barmouth Estuary, which is well placed if you are arriving by train or prefer to separate the route into two circuits.

2. Ride south through Dolgellau past the church, and then take the road signposted to Cadair Idris. This starts with a long, steady uphill as it leaves the town, soon pulling out into open country. Ignore all side turnings and ride on past Llyn Gwernan, where you will find a pub and hotel in an attractive setting.

3. Past Llyn Gwernan the road drops down to cross a stream by a car park. The track that runs by the side of the car park is a bridleway (no signpost) that leads through to the Youth Hostel at Kings Dolgellau, though once the track comes to an end I found it difficult to follow. The next right turn off the road also leads through to the Youth Hostel, which is pleasantly situated in a thickly wooded valley with the road running on eventually to join the A493. It makes for an extremely pretty ride, and if you have the time is well worth exploring.

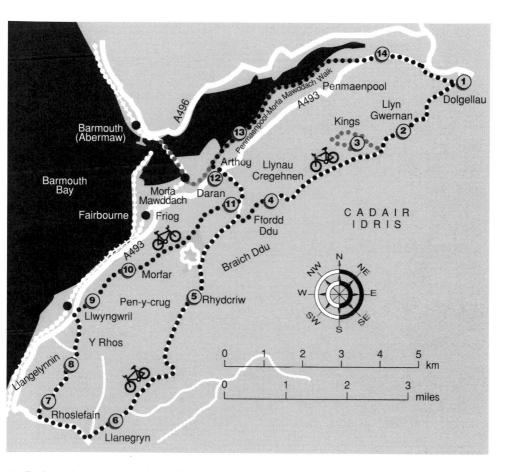

4. Back on the main route, the road continues beneath the huge mass of Cadair Idris, coming to the turn-off for the lake at Lynnau Cregennen. Carry straight on here, and look out for a track going off to the left, which starts with a short patch of tarmac. This is start of the track that heads up Ffordd Ddu and is the way to continue the hill and coast circuit. If you prefer to confine your ride to the Dolgellau and railway circuit, ignore this track and ride straight on, taking the next right turn in the road, which goes steeply downhill to join the old railway at Arthog at Stage 11 of the full route.

5. The track up Ffordd Ddu leads into the old road that goes up and over the top of the hills at Rhydcriw before dropping down to the sea. Some of it is tarmac while other parts are rough, but it is easy to ride on even when it is a steady grind uphill. Near the top you pass a clump of isolated forestry, and then by a sheep pen start a massive downhill that is tarmac all the way as the narrow road twists and turns on the drop into the valley of the Afon Dysynni.

6. Keep right along the road for Llanegryn, and then turn right onto the main A493 for Rhoslefain. It may be an A road, but it is not unpleasant to ride just over a mile on.

7. At Rhoslefain you could keep on along the A493 for Llwyngwril, but the more interesting option is to take the direct hill route. Turn right at the crossroads opposite the turning for the station, and follow the narrow lane uphill past Llabwst Farm. Ignore the left turn, which is a dead-end, and carry on through the gate past Craig-fadyn, still climbing to the high point where you will come to the dilapidated barns at Pant-gwyn. This is where the new-style OS map shows a 'route with public access' heading over the hills towards Rhydcriw, and at least some of this route can be seen on the ground.

8. From Pant-gwyn the lane starts to drop downhill with only the occasional gate to slow your progress. Ignore the left turning, which goes steeply down to rejoin the A493, and keep right to emerge on the A493 on the outskirts of Llwyngwril.

9. Ride into Llwyngwril on the A493, crossing the bridge over the Afon Gwril and taking the second turn to the right near the pub – it is a tricky turning off the main road, so take care. This is correctly signposted as a dead-end road, heading steeply up the hillside as it passes a few houses on the outskirts of the village, before heading out into open country at Hendre. For the next 2 miles (3km) it is shown as a 'route with public access'. The narrow road winds its way steeply up the hillside between high stone walls, before leaving civilization behind at the farmstead at Parth-y-gwyddwch where it joins a grass track that goes extra-steeply uphill and then levels out to follow the high contours with fine views out over Barmouth Bay and Estuary.

10. Once you have made the climb this track is easy riding, and all too soon the grass comes to an end and tarmac takes over once again when you drop down to join the entrance drive to Cefnfeusydd Farm. From here the narrow tarmac lane winds its way up and down towards the forestry beneath Pen y Garn, giving an excellent ride through fine terrain. The route passes a few houses at Bron-llety-Ifan, and then heads uphill thorough an extraordinary stone landscape above Daran, before finally levelling out on a long straight and then dropping down to a gate.

11. Go through this gate and turn left steeply downhill for Arthog. Watch out for the gate half-way down; the narrow road is steep and gets even steeper, delivering you back on the A493 below Craig-bwch at Arthog.

12. Watching for traffic, turn briefly right along the A493, taking the first left turn through a gate to join a lane that crosses the old Penmaenpool–Morfa railway. You reach the railway at a bridge where you would turn left for Morfa Mawddach station. This is approximately one mile (1.5km) to the west and gives the option of riding across Barmouth bridge and into Barmouth itself. Dolgellau is approximately 8 miles (13km) to the east.

13. As railway paths go, the Penmaenpool–Morfa line offers very pleasant riding, following the side of the wide Barmouth Estuary on a cinder surface that is easy enough to ride without encouraging the excess speed that will cause altercations with the walkers and strollers who also use the line.

14. At Penmaenpool you come to the toll bridge that crosses to the other side, but the way is straight on, passing the pub and reaching the end of the old railway close by the junction of the A493 and A494. Turn right onto the A493 here for a short distance, taking the first left turn after the bridge and following this road for about a mile by the side of the Afon Wnion back into Dolgellau.

Places To Visit:
Welsh Gold Centre at Dolgellau (tel: 01341 423332);
Ruins of Cymmer Abbey (Cadw – tel: 01341 422854), near Llanelltyd north of Dolgellau.

Pubs and Cafés:
Pubs and cafés at Dolgellau;
pubs along the route at Llyn Gwernan, Llwyngwril and Penmaenpool.

16 Round Coed-y-Brenin Forest Park

Area: Gwynedd – a tour of the Coed-y-Brenin Forest Park on the A470 to the north of Dolgellau. Start and finish at Coed-y-Brenin Visitor Centre on the west side of the A470 near the northern edge of the forest.

OS Map: Landranger 124 – Dolgellau.

Route:
Coed-y-Brenin Visitor Centre car park (GR:714277)
Coed Dôl-gefeiliau (GR:717270)
Ty-newydd-gwyllt (GR:718255)
Ganllwyd/A470 (GR:727243)
A470/Ty'n-y-groes (GR:730233)
Glasdir (GR:736227)
Dôl-frwynog (GR:744256)
Moel Hafodowen (GR:757267)
Dôl-frwynog (GR:744256)
Afon Mawddach (GR:735251)
Pont Dôl-gefeiliau/A470 (GR:719275)
Coed-y-Brenin Visitor Centre car park (GR:714277)

Nearest BR station: No main line station within easy reach.

Nearest Youth Hostel: Kings Dolgellau at GR:648603 to the west of Dolgellau; Ffestiniog at GR:704427 near Ffestiniog.

Approx length: Up to 22 miles (35km) on Expert Route.

Time: Allow 3 to 4 hours.

Rating: Moderate to hard. If you want to storm around the Expert Route, there are plenty of demanding hills as well as some interesting technical sections. The Sport Route also has plenty of hills, so do not underestimate it.

Dedicated mountain bike routes through forestry do not generally appeal to me, but the purpose-designed routes through the Coed-y-Brenin Forest Park are an exception. This large mass of forestry has more interesting topography than many of its rivals, and the three dedicated mountain bike routes are cleverly designed to give some real variety and be a hard challenge for those who aim to complete the most taxing 'Expert Route'.

1. If time permits, the official forest routes could be mixed and matched with several bridleways that pass through the forest, and even linked into Ride 23 by using the track that the OS describes as a 'route with public access' from the Sarn Helen Roman Kilns (GR: 727317) to the heart of the forest route or the minor road that crosses the Afon Mawddach at Pont Aber-Geirw. There are lots of opportunities here for those who are handy with a map, but even by sticking to the official routes you are guaranteed some excellent riding that can be mixed and matched according to your inclinations and ability, the weather and the time available.

2. There are three official routes – 35km Expert, 22km Sport and 11km Fun – clearly shown on a map leaflet issued by the Park Centre or available from the Dolgellau Forest District. All the routes start together, heading steeply uphill from the Forest Centre, and then turning left onto a rough forest road with a no-entry sign – this seems confusing at first, but you soon get used to following the appropriate coloured arrows.

3. From here all three routes start to move quite steeply up the hillside, moving onto single track and emerging at the top with fine views over the valley. The riding is excellent, with a variety of tracks that are much more fun that the usual wide forest roads, with plenty of broadleaf trees to break up the usual monotony of pine forestry. The route map itself has some useful symbols to tell

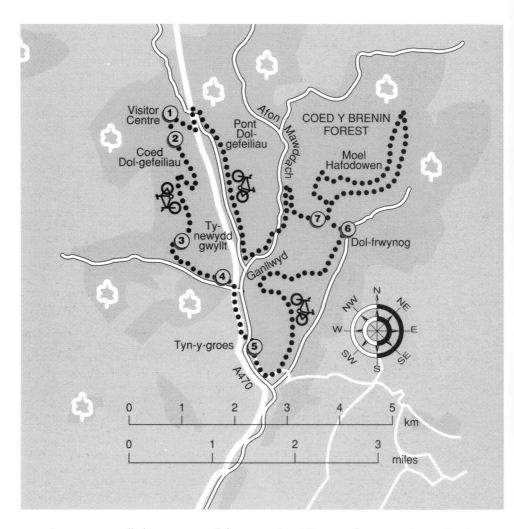

you what to expect all the way – a sad face for uphills, a happy face for downhills, and others to show such features as rocky, technical or wet sections – and these are augmented by useful short cut signs for those on the Fun Route.

4. While the Fun Route loops back to the start, both the Expert and Sport Route continue down to the road, with the Expert Route visiting the first of three technical sections to be encountered – I missed this one

by riding too fast, or perhaps the signpost was missing. On the way downhill they join a narrow tarmac track that passes a splendid stretch of wild, cascading river (in the right season), and then you are out on the A470 where you turn south for a short distance to pick up the routes on the east side of the forest at the Ty'n-y-groes bridge.

5. Coed-y-Brenin east of the A470 is much more of the traditional style of endless, uniform fir forest with wide, fast roads, but the

Watch the arrows and you can't go far wrong. Coed-y-Brenin offers fine riding in pleasant surroundings with a surprisingly tough Expert Circuit.

on forestry roads to the north that is eventually rewarded by some big views and a big downhill featuring some interestingly sharp bends that will make anyone feel like a downhill star. The Expert Route then goes into its third and final technical section, but shortly before this I made the decision to change down from Expert to Sport. The forest roads are dark towards the end of an autumn day, and I did not fancy a technical ride through even denser gloom. As I had started the ride late it was time to take the quickest route back to the Visitor Centre.

7. After an easy uphill it seemed a very long downhill to the bridge that crosses the Afon Mawddach, with a steady, mainly downhill ride all the way back to the Visitor Centre. Despite changing routes I had covered almost 20 miles (32km), and having been tired at the start from a taxing 40 mile (65km) ride in the morning had taken almost three hours over it. The Coed-y-Brenin forest routes are not to be underestimated – allow plenty of time, take both the forest map and the OS map, and you can create your own variations with the potential for making it a very full day out.

cycle routes are nevertheless interesting and fairly taxing. After following a minor road round the perimeter of the forest, the Expert Route leaves the Sport Route to go off on a high loop with high views ending with a technical section that takes you along a sometimes tricky single track in the dark, dense woods. Both routes then rejoin on the tarmac road at Dôl-frwynog.

6. From Dôl-frwynog the Expert Route heads off once again, with a long, steep climb

---

Places To Visit:
Coed-y-Brenin Visitor Centre, including shop and bike hire (tel: 01766 87569).

Pubs and Cafés:
Café at the Visitor Centre;
Ty'n-y groes Hotel on the A470 at south end of route.

17 Mynydd Mawr Circuit

Area: The Berwyn Hills to the west of Oswestry via Llanarmon Dyffryn Ceiriog and Llangadwaladr. Start and finish at Llanrhaeadr-ym-Mochnant on the B4580 12 miles (20km) west of Oswestry. Car park in the village.

OS Map: Landranger 125 – Bala and Lake Vyrnwy.

Route:
Llanrhaeadr-ym-Mochnant (GR:123261)
Cefn-y-rhodfa (GR:123307)
Llanarmon Dyffryn Ceiriog
(GR:158328)
Ty'n-y-fedw (GR:172326)
Ty-gwyn (GR:178299)
Preswylfa (GR:155292)
Llanarmon Mynydd-mawr (GR:145277)
Llanrhaeadr-ym-Mochnant
(GR:123261)

Nearest BR Station:
None within easy reach.

Nearest Youth Hostel:
Cynwyd on the west side of the Berwyn wilderness at GR:057409. Llangollen to the north-east at GR:232413.

Approx Length: 13 miles (21km).

Time: Allow around 2–3 hours.

Rating: Easy to moderate. Much of this circuit is on-road with lots of ups and downs. The short offroad section is potentially strenuous. Extending the ride across the wilderness towards the River Dee would make it a serious, long-distance ride.

This can be linked to the ride across the Berwyn wilderness (Ride 20). It follows a delightful route on a mainly on-road switchback of narrow lanes through forgotten countryside with some brilliant views, and makes a highly recommended short circuit for those who like to take it quite easy.

1. Llanrhaeadr-ym-Mochnant is a village well away from any big towns, and right on the edge of an impressive area of wilderness. With the Afon Rhaeadr flowing through its middle it is a delightful one-street place that appears to have quite a lot going on, with a choice of pubs and cafés to choose from, plus several bed and breakfast places if you want to stay overnight. From the small car park on the east side of the village head uphill past the police station, and then take the first turn on the left. This leads north on a narrow country lane, taking you up and down through really beautiful countryside as you follow the side of the Afon Iwrch.

2. Take the right-hand fork at Tan-y-ffridd, steadily gaining height, and going right again at Tyn-y-ffridd where there is a large farmstead. A moderately serious uphill takes you onto the ridge to the south of Garneddwen. When I pedalled along here in mid-April there was deep snow with more to come – but the views were still pretty good, with the Berwyn wilderness stretching to the north.

3. At the end of the ridge the road leads steeply down towards Llanarmon Dyffryn Ceiriog. This is a great descent, and with few cars around you can really go for it. Llanarmon Dyffryn Ceiriog is a charming little place blessed with a small village shop and post office, two pubs and a church by the side of the Afon Ceiriog, though one suspects it may be popular with car-borne trippers in summer. From here you can join Ride 18 by striking out across the Berwyn wilderness, following the dead end lane signposted to Pentre.

4. To continue the circuit back to Llanrhaeadr-ym-Mochnant the route leads steeply

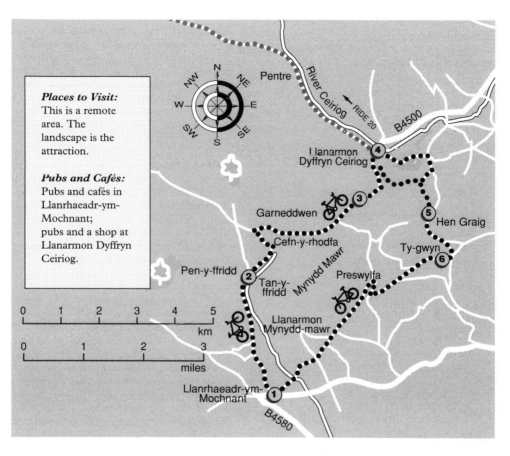

uphill on the south side of the Afon Ceiriog, and then turns off on a track that leads south across the hilltops towards the summit of Hen Graig. In better weather purist mountain bikers should stick with the official bridleway, which heads steeply up the hillside on the south-west side of Llanarmon Dyffryn Ceiriog, joining the track close by Hen Graig.

5. Navigation is not easy here; keep on the west side of Hen Graig and follow the track down the steep hillside to a sheep pen (you are in big sheep country), joining a track that follows a stream towards The Lawnt farmstead. It can be muddy here, and with hawthorns on both sides it is also a likely place to puncture, as I discovered.

6. Follow the track out onto the road by Ty-gwyn. Some interesting bridleway tracks head eastwards from here if you want to go exploring offroad, while narrow country lanes lead back towards Llanrhaeadr-ym-Mochnant, winding and wriggling their way through the hills with plenty of ups and downs; in particular there is a very good downhill as you pass the small chapel on the hillside above Preswylfa. From here it is around 3 miles (5km) back to the starting point at Llanrhaeadr-ym-Mochnant where there are some interesting possibilities for making up your own offroad circuit on the bridleways that head round the west side of Moel Hen-fache just over a mile north of the village.

18 Llangollen Canal and Ridge Ride

Offroad and On-Road

Area: Clwyd – a tour of the high ground to the south of Llangollen, returning by the Shropshire Union Canal and the famous Pont Cysyllte aqueduct. Start and finish at Llangollen on the A5.

OS Map: OS Map: Landranger 117 – Chester, Wrexham & surrounding area.

Route:
Llangollen (GR:215418)
Plas Newydd (GR:220417)
Ty'n-Celyn (GR:234412)
Radio mast (GR:249404)
Fron Isaf (GR:271405)
A5 (GR:278409)
Froncysyllte (GR:270413)
Pont Cysyllte aqueduct (GR:271420)
Shropshire Union Canal (GR:240425)
Llangollen (GR:215418)

Nearest BR Station: Chirk.

Nearest Youth Hostel: Llangollen.

Approx length: 12 miles (19km).

Time: Allow 2 hours.

Rating: Moderate. The offroad climb to the top of the ridge on the south side of the Vale of Llangollen is hard, but from there on it is easy pedalling.

This route makes a fine companion to Ride 19 (which explores the Horseshoe Pass) and is particularly handy for the Llan-gollen Youth Hostel. Whether it is best tackled anti-clockwise or clockwise is open to question – while an anticlockwise circuit has the disadvantage of a very hard offroad climb, an easy section of Shropshire Union Canal makes a pleasant way to finish.

1. From the centre of Llangollen turn left onto the A5 going east, and after a short distance fork right off the A5 following the signpost to Plas Newydd. Follow the road past this fine old house, which has now been turned into a museum, and ride out into farmland on the road that follows the side of the hill in an arc beneath the tree-covered ridge high above.

2. At the centre of the arc ride on past the entrance to the farmstead at Tan-y-graig, and continue past the entrance to Ty'n-Celyn where a sign advertises bed and breakfast. Where the road bends left – leading direct to the Llan-gollen Youth Hostel at Tyndwr Hall, a short way off – turn right through a gate up a steep rough track, ignoring the smooth track that goes straight ahead signposted as a footpath.

3. Follow the track uphill, with forestry on the right and open ground on the left. Look for the clear track that is the byway bearing off to the left, and follow it across the hillside. At first it is a hard climb, but it eventually levels out and gets steadier with fine views opening out over the Vale of Llangollen and glimpses of the Pont Cysyllte aqueduct some way ahead.

4. At the top of the hill the track joins a minor road running down from the top of the ridge. Turn left here, following the road straight ahead on a long and fast downhill that leads to Fron Isaf. Follow the road round to the right here, and then by the telephone box take a left and left again to follow a narrow lane that goes north to join the A5.

5. There are two options here. The straightforward route is to turn left along the A5 and ride

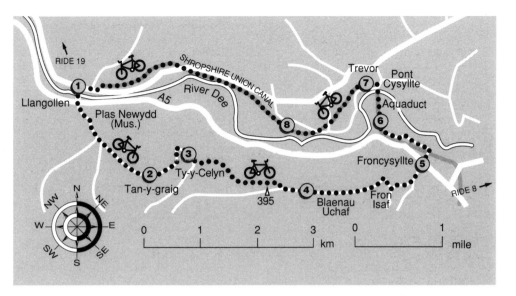

the short distance into Froncysyllte, turning right off the A5 from Trevor, which brings you steeply down to the Shropshire Union Canal. Alternatively, you can cross straight over the A5, and if no one objects follow the lane, which dips under and then runs along the side of the canal before joining the canal path at Froncysyllte.

6. British Waterways say that you can ride your bike all the way from Irish bridge (bridge 27) to Llangollen, but you should have a permit and may only walk your bike over the Pont Cysyllte aqueduct. To cross the aqueduct join the canal path on the north side of the canal, and be prepared for the amazing sensation of crossing high in the air above the Vale of Llangollen with only a canal for company.

7. On the north side the Shropshire Union Canal splits, with the main waterway heading north while the Llangollen branch heads west. Ride off the canal and over the bridge, turning left and right to get onto the Llangollen branch, which necessitates changing from the right bank to the left bank after a short distance.

8. Riding the 5 miles (8km) or so along the canal is easy and pleasant riding, though you should be prepared for some very muddy sections after wet weather. Close to Llangollen you can expect to encounter walkers and strollers, so do the right thing by slowing down and giving way whenever you come across them.

Places To Visit:
Llangollen Railway (tel: 01978 860951) runs between Llangollen and Glyndyfrdwy;
Remains of Vale Crucis Abbey (Cadw – tel: 01978 860362);
Llangollen Wharf (tel: 01978 860702);
Llangollen Motor Museum (tel: 01978 860324);
Victorian School and Museum (tel: 01978 860794);
Canoe Centre (tel: 01978 860763);
Plas Newydd – once home of 'the ladies of Llangollen' on the outskirts of the town.

Pubs and Cafés:
Pubs and cafés at Llangollen;
pubs at Froncysyllte and at the Shropshire Union canal junction at the north end of the Pont Cysyllte aqueduct.

19 The Llangollen Horseshoe

On-Road

Area: Clwyd – a tour of the famous Horseshoe Pass and the Llantysilio Mountain area to the west of Llangollen. Start and finish at Llangollen on the A5.

OS Map: Landranger 117 – Chester, Wrexham & surrounding area. Landranger 116 – Denbigh & Colwyn Bay area. Landranger 126 – Shrewsbury & surrounding area.

Route:
Llangollen (GR:215418)
A542/Pen-y-clawdd farm (GR:202457)
Old Horseshoe road/A542 (GR:192482)
A514 via minor road (GR:163484)
A514 turn-off (GR:159482)
Bwlch y Groes (GR:147456)
Craig-y-Rhos (GR:147437)
Efenechtyd (GR:166435)
Rhewl (GR:180448)
Llantysilio Hall/B5103 (GR:198433)
Llangollen (GR:215418)

Nearest BR Station: Chirk.

Nearest Youth Hostel:
Llangollen

Approx Length: 17¹/₂ miles (28km).

Time: Allow 2 hours.

Rating: Moderate. It is a hard climb up to the Horseshoe Pass, but the riding is easy and very enjoyable thereafter.

Llangollen is a busy place with many attractions that include the international Eisteddfod and the River Dee rushing through its centre. It is set in the midst of fine hills, with the famous Horseshoe Pass winding majestically between the Maesyrchen and Llantysilio mountains. This is a fine tour of the area, best undertaken when there are few car-borne tourists about. For those who have the legs, it can also be linked to Ride 18.

1. There are a number of car parks in Llangollen; alternatively you could start this ride from the car park at the top of the Horseshoe Pass. Find your way to the centre of Llangollen, crossing the bridge over the River Dee from south to north. Turn left past the old station, and then follow the A542 out of town heading north.

2. When I rode it the A542 was quiet and quite acceptable for cycling, but in the busy summer season it could be another matter. You have got about 2 miles (3km) to ride along it, passing the remains of Vale Crucis Abbey, which are worth a visit, and then starting on a steady uphill where a path that follows the roadside could be useful if cars become an annoyance. Look out for a hotel on the left side of the road where it bends, and then take the next right turn off the A542 onto a narrow country lane.

3. This is the old Horseshoe Pass road, and much more pleasant to ride on. It follows the same direction as the A542 but stays farther down the hillside, before a very long and steep uphill brings you to the top with huge views to the east in fine and wild surroundings. Riding up here is quite a challenge, with the road only levelling out as it once again approaches the A542.

4. At the top a local had recommended trying the track that leads to the radio masts, and from there following tracks farther east before descending on the minor road that heads due south. However the track had a gate with a

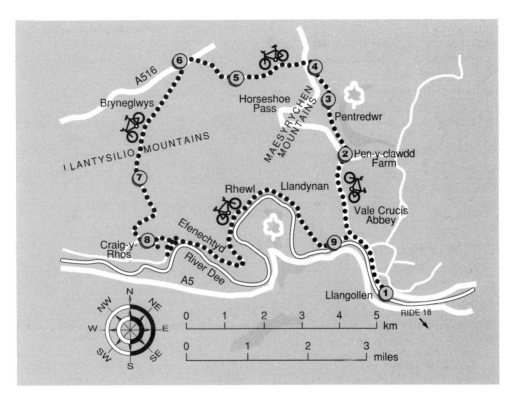

terrifying battery of padlocks, indicating that it is certainly not a right of way and cannot be recommended.

5. Instead I crossed straight over the A542, joining the narrow road that heads west round the side of the Llantysilio Mountain, steadily heading downhill as it weaves its way to join up with the A5104 some 2 miles (3km) distant on the lowlands. There is a bridleway option here. It cuts along the tops of the hills, and is shown as starting at the first house on a tight hairpin bend. Either I was going too fast or it was not obvious, and I opted to stay with the road, which if car-free is highly enjoyable.

6. Turn left along the A5104 for a short distance, and then take the next left turn off it, following a lane that heads up round the hillside. If you wish to divert to the pub at Bryneglwys you should take the first right turn; otherwise carry on, steadily and easily gaining height round the side of the mountain and carrying straight on at the junction at Bwlch y Groes.

7. From here the views are stupendous and there are some magnificent downhill sections as the road hugs the sides of the mountains on its way southwards. Do not take the right turn on a hairpin bend, which leads down to a farm and a dead-end (footpath connection only), but keep on with the road to take the next left fork with a slight climb over high ground at Craig-y-Rhos. Alternatively, carry straight on down the hill for Glyndyfrdwy if you want to go straight into Ride 18.

8. From Craig-y-Rhos you come to a farm that at first looks like a dead-end, but the road carries on right through the middle and leads steeply down the hillside to the hamlet at the

The area around Llangollen is very hilly but offers some brilliant views when you hit the top. This is what it looks like from the south side.

bottom by the riverside. Turn left here, and follow the road by the side of the River Dee as it twists and turns on its way east down to Llangollen. It is not all easy riding as the road rises and falls on the hillside, passing the Sun Inn at Rhewl before eventually joining the B5103 about a mile from Llangollen.

9. The B5103 soon runs into the A542, along which you can retrace your wheeltracks back to Llangollen. The latter part of the route also runs alongside the Llangollen branch of the Shropshire Union Canal, which local cyclists make use of to get off the road, but only the section between Llangollen (bridge 45) and Irish bridge to the east is promoted by British Waterways as being open to cyclists who are also asked to display a permit.

Places To Visit:
Llangollen Railway (tel: 01978 860951) runs between Llangollen and Glyndyfrdwy;
Remains of Vale Crucis Abbey (Cadw – tel: 01978 860362);
Llangollen Wharf (tel: 01978 860702);
Llangollen Motor Museum (tel: 01978 860324);
Victorian School and Museum (tel: 01978 860794);
Canoe Centre (tel: 01978 860763);
Plas Newydd – once home of 'the ladies of Llangollen' on the outskirts of the town.

Pubs and Cafés:
Pubs and cafés at Llangollen; café at the top of the Horseshoe Pass; pubs on the A542 road 2 miles (3km) north of Llangollen, at Bryneglwys (off-route on the A5104), and at Rhewl.

20 The Wayfarer's Route

Area: Clwyd – a double crossing of the Berwyn Hills to the south of the A5 west of Llangollen. Start and finish at Corwen on the A5.

OS Map: OS Maps: Landranger 125 – Bala and Lake Vyrnwy. Landranger 126 – Shrewsbury & surrounding area.

Route:
Corwen (GR:075436)
Carrog (GR:105437)
Glyndyfrdwy/A5 (GR:149426)
Ceiriog forest (GR:155388)
Glyn Ceiriog/B4500 (GR:203381)
Tregeiriog/B4500 (GR:177338)
Llanarmon Dyffryn Ceiriog/B4500 (GR:157328)
Pentre (GR:136348)
Wayfarer Memorial (GR:091367)
B4401/Cynwyd (GR:056410)
Corwen (GR:075436)

Nearest BR Station: Chirk.

Nearest Youth Hostel: Cynwyd.

Approx Length: 30 miles (48km).

Time: Allow 5 hours.

Rating: Moderate to hard. It is a good distance with plenty of steady climbs. Riding it all the way would deserve a 'hard' rating. If you are prepared to get off and push on some of the longest hills it is 'moderate'.

This superb ride makes two crossings of the Berwyn Hills, follows the Wayfarer's Road and explores the delightful north banks of the River Dee. It is a 'must' for a fine, still day, and can be linked to Ride 21 for those who want an even bigger circuit.

1. Corwen makes a good place to start this ride, with a choice of car parks in this village about 9 miles (14km) west of Llangollen along the A5. Alternatively you could start from Cynwyd, which has roadside parking available at the crossroads, or at Glyndyfrdwy where there is a convenient lay-by on the A5 a short distance east of the route.

2. Take the road from the centre of Corwen that is signposted to the industrial estate. At first this seems fairly unpromising, heading south to cross the River Dee, after which it comes up to a large T-junction. Turn right along the B5437 for Carrog here, and enjoy pedalling as the road gradually transforms.

3. Before long the B5437 has narrowed down into a very minor road, following the hillside through delightful countryside with few cars likely to bother you. Carrog is a splendid place, with its houses leaning over the River Dee, and from here you join an even more minor road instead of crossing the river.

4. Keep pedalling due east as far as Coed Iâl where you come to the second bridge across the Dee. Cross the river here, and ride over the Llangollen Railway at the crossing – it may be possible to get your bike here by train from Llangollen – before riding up to the A5 at Glyndyfrdwy. Turn left along the A5 for a short distance, looking out for a narrow right turn by the side of a chapel marked as being unsuitable for cars, which is the way you want to go.

5. The old road leads uphill and through a gate on a rough surface, heading up through trees before breaking out on the hillside above the Nant y Pandy stream. Some of the road is tarmac but much has been washed away, and as you steadily gain height the views get more stupen-

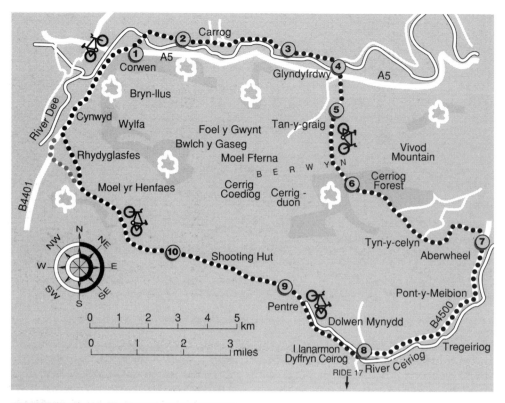

The Wayfarer Memorial is now sadly scratched by vandals.

dous with a fairly easy slope to get you to the top if you do not mind a long climb.

6. Once you are on top the road starts to head down into the Ceiriog forest. From here it is a fast and steady downhill on the forest road, taking you past a secluded car park and onto a very minor country road. Ignore all left turnings for Chirk, and instead keep right to follow the road to Glyn Ceiriog, which is eventually reached after a long and fairly dramatic downhill as the road zigzags into the valley.

7. From Glyn Ceiriog turn right along the B4500, and follow this country road west to the hamlet of Llanarmon Dyffryn Ceiriog. At first there is a steady uphill out of Glyn Ceiriog, but the road eventually levels out and becomes easy riding, following the course of the Afon Ceiriog until it enters Llanarmon Dyffryn Ceiriog with its choice of two pubs facing one another at the crossroads and a link with Ride 21.

8. From Llanarmon Dyffryn Ceiriog turn right along the dead-end lane signposted to Pentre and Rhiw. After passing a few houses, a track

Spoilt for choice! The crossroads of Llanarmon Dyffryn Ceiriog offers two public houses before the offroad climb.

takes over from the tarmac by the last house at Swch-cae-rhiw, and from here you are on the old Wayfarer's Road – 'Wayfarer' was the pseudonym of an early offroader who was later celebrated as the inspiration for the Rough-Stuff Fellowship, a group of offroad cyclists who first formed their club in the 1950s long before mountain bikes appeared.

9. The track that follows is ridable all the way across the Berwyn Hills, though there are some tricky sections and much of the way is a steady uphill. The spectacular, steep-sided valley of the Afon Ceiriog is soon left behind, as the track crosses desolate moor where in wet weather you may find much of the surface under water. Most of the old road is in fairly good condition and will continue to be so if it can avoid the destructive excesses of the four-wheel-drive fraternity, though mountain bikers also have a responsibility to take care how they ride on these old roads. The only blot on the horizon is a patch of forestry dumped into the middle of the landscape with total lack of regard for its environmental and visual impact, and a little way on a short climb takes you to the pass where you will find the Wayfarer Memorial set in the rocks of the hillside.

10. From the Wayfarer Memorial follow the track downhill, keeping right all the way. It is mainly a fast descent all the way, indeed so fast that I managed to miss the right fork that should lead direct to Cynwyd, and instead found myself out on the B4401 at Rhydyglafes about one mile south-west of the village. No matter; if you end up here turn right and it is an easy pedal along the road to Cynwyd and beyond, turning right along the A5 for a short distance to get back to the starting point at Corwen at the end of a truly memorable ride. (If you prefer to miss out the A5, look out for the back road, which connects the B4401 with the Corwen crossroads.)

Places to Visit:
Llangollen Railway (tel: 01978 860951) runs between Llangollen and Glyndyfrdwy.

Pubs and Cafés:
Pubs and cafés at Corwen; pubs at Glyndyfrdwy, Glyn Ceiriog, Llanarmon Dyffryn Ceiriog and Cynwyd.

21 Llandrillo and the Berwyn Hills

This is an extremely pleasant circuit using minor roads, old roads and bridle-ways to climb up the sides of the valleys from the River Dee east of Bala. It would become difficult to follow only in wet weather or poor visibility.

1. You could start the ride from Bala or its nearby Youth Hostel, using the B4401 to join the route. Alternatively you can park a car at a convenient lay-by on the B4391 by the side of the woods just south of the turn-off that goes steeply downhill towards Llandderfel, or in the village of Llandrillo.

2. From Llandderfel turn right on a minor road in the centre of the village. Follow this on an easy uphill past a few houses, forking left before you come to a converted Welsh chapel on the hillside. From here the dead-end road gets narrower and steeper, climbing up the side of the valley with good views opening out to the south.

3. When you come to a track going straight ahead at Garth-lwyd, turn hard left to follow the road fairly steeply uphill. Ride on past the driveways to the farmsteads at Cae-pant and Bryn-derw, passing a signposted bridle-way track that turns off to the north. Here you keep straight on ahead to the end of the tar-mac road, passing the entrance to Hafoty Wen and going through a gate to join a rough but reasonable track.

4. This track follows a steady uphill, passing close to a remote and idyllic looking cottage at Cistfaen. Here the track splits two ways round a hummock; I was advised to take the right-hand track, which follows the south side of the hummock, bearing round to the left before joining a fairly distinct track that heads on across the wild moorland of Mynydd Mynyllod. Mostly it is fairly easy to follow and to ride, with wheel tracks through the heather showing the way past strange rock piles. At the end of the moor the route leads through a gate, and then on down the side of a field to join a hard track near the southern corner of

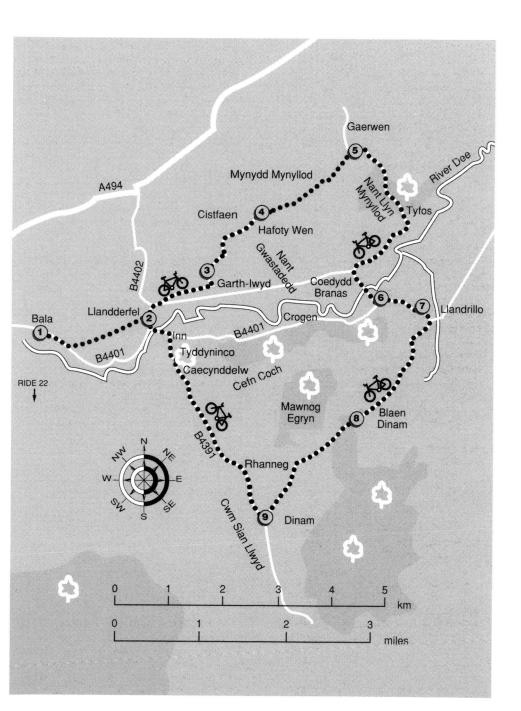

the woodland by Gaerwen.

5. Turn right to go eastward along this track, which offers good and fairly fast riding. Passing below a steep hill it enters more forestry by the Nant Llyn Mynyllod river, where a good downhill soon leads to the road by Tyfos. Turn right to head south-west here, taking the first left turn to cross the River Dee and join the B4401.

6. Turn left on the B4401 and ride on to Llandrillo, a small place where you might find something to amuse you. If you have time on your side and plenty of reserve leg power, this could include a tour of the forestry above the village, which has a bridleway and road loop giving what looks like a most convenient ride.

7. To follow the main route, turn right off the B4401 as you enter the village, leaving the church on your left and riding on to where the road splits. The left fork might be an interesting option, leading along the Cwm Pennant and from there up through forestry, but the right fork is the way that this route goes. At first it appears to head towards a housing estate, but from here the road becomes more interesting, heading up the hillside and entering the woods by Blaen Dinam where the tarmac disappears.

8. From here the road continues south-west

to the top of the Berwyn Hills. Parts still have tarmac but much of it is washed away, which makes it ideal for a bike with a steady climb and little chance of meeting any motor vehicles. At the top the road deteriorates still further; follow it through a gate past a small patch of forestry, and from here on to join the B4391.

9. Turn right along the B4391 to head north. A steady downhill will soon bring you across the cattle grid to a patch of forestry on the right where there is a convenient lay-by to leave a car. A short distance past here look out for the right turn into the trees, which is not signposted. This follows a very narrow lane, which soon plunges very steeply downhill to join the road by the pub at Pale. Turn left here to cross the River Dee, turning left towards Bala if that is where you started the ride.

Places To Visit:
Bala Lake Railway along the south shore of Lake Bala.

Pubs and Cafés:
Pubs and cafés at Bala; pubs along the route at Pale and Llandrillo.

22 Big Bala Circuit

Mainly On-Road

Area: Gwynedd and Clwyd – a double circuit to the south and north-west of Bala. Start and finish at Bala on the A494.

OS Maps: Landranger 125 – Bala and Lake Vyrnwy. Landranger 124 – Dolgellau.

Route:
First circuit
Bala car park (GR:930363)
B4391/Rhos-y-gwaliau (GR:943347)
Cwm Hirnant/Penllyn forest (GR:953313)
Braich-yr Owen (GR:962252)
Ffridd Wydd-afon/New bridge (GR:964242)
Pont Eunant/Lake Vyrnwy (GR:963225)
Bwlch Groes (GR:914228)
Cwm Cynllwyd (GR:900267)
Pandy/B4403 (GR:882299)
Bala car park (GR:930363)
Second circuit
Bala car park (GR:930363)
B4403/Pandy (GR:882299)
A494/Dothendre (GR:853310)
Blaenlliw Isaf (GR:806335)
Pont y Gain (GR:751327)
A470/Trawsfynydd/A4212 (GR:711355)
A4212/B4391 (GR:816395)
Llidiardau (GR:873383)
Rhyd-uchaf (GR:903379)
Bala car park (GR:930363)

Nearest BR Station: None within easy reach.

Nearest Youth Hostel: Bala at GR:947348.

Approx Length: First circuit 28 miles (45km); second circuit 35 miles (56km); combined circuit 54 miles (87km).

Time: Allow 3 hours for the first circuit; 4 to 5 hours for the second circuit; a full day for the combined circuit.

Rating: There are plenty of climbs so care needs to be taken to conserve energy. Going offroad makes the ride considerably more arduous and will increase the time factor.

The area around Lake Bala is particularly attractive, and renowned for its narrow, hilly roads that are so much better suited to bikes than cars. If you take care to ride here away from the main season you can expect to have these roads pretty much to yourself, with the option of offroad excursions giving extra interest to these two fine circuits that can be ridden separately or combined into one grand tour of the area.

First circuit

1. Bala is a pleasant town at the north-east corner of the lake that takes its name. Its attractions include a wide selection of shops, which include a friendly bike shop at the east end of the town, while the Information Centre, located out of town westwards along the A494, is also worth a visit. There is a large car park on the eastern fringes of the town where the B4391 crosses the A494, which makes a convenient place to start from.

2. You can either follow the B4391 south, or ride into town and take the left turn from the centre that follows the same direction closer to the shores of the lake. Turn left on the B4402 signposted for Llandrillo, riding uphill away from the lake and taking the first right turn signposted for Bala Youth Hostel. Follow the narrow road up the

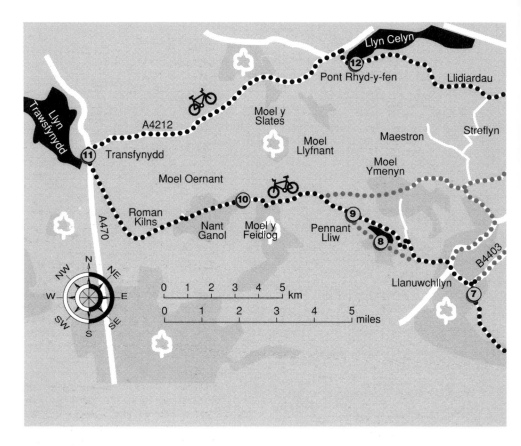

hillside, and from there down to the bridge at Rhos-y-gwaliau. Turn left across the bridge; the Bala Youth Hostel is up the hill to the left here, a fine Welsh stone building that makes a good base from which to explore the neighbourhood.

3. From Rhos-y-gwaliau a delightful ride south along Cwm Hirnant follows the narrow road on easy ups and downs with the gushing river on the right and the Penllyn forest rising up the hillsides on the left. You can follow this road all the way to Lake Vyrnwy, or indulge in an offroad section round the Penllyn forest that was recommended to me as 'the local mountain bike circuit' by both the Bala bike shop and the warden of the youth hostel. However it is not a right of way, and while it is a very fine circuit you should enquire locally

(with particular regard to the southern part of the track) before setting off on it.

The offroad turn-off comes at a sharp right turn in the road about 3 miles (5km) past the Youth Hostel. The route follows a forestry road straight ahead here, keeping left to head south-east on a steady uphill by the side of Nant Ystrad-y-groes. Heading towards the high point of 2,160ft (659m) the route joins a rougher, narrower forestry track, still climbing before breaking out of the forestry at a gate and joining a track that dips, dives and weaves round the hillsides on the tops of open ground with famous views on all sides. This steadily bears round to the west to pass Pen y Boncyn Trefeilw, before dropping fairly steeply to re-join the road at the end of this 60-minute excursion.

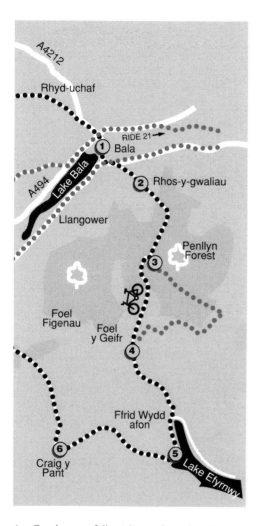

and steep, and so long as there are few cars about is the epitome of fine on-road cycling. It climbs by the side of the River Eunant, passing waterfalls and wrecked buildings, before leaving the trees and heading out through an area of wilderness with a steady climb beyond Y Gadfa.

6. About 4 miles (6km) from Lake Vyrnwy you reach a road junction by a cross and a memorial, with huge views to the south and an even more huge downhill to the valley. However here you turn right (north), following the narrow road a short distance uphill to the pass, before starting a long and memorable downhill along Cwm Cynllwyd. This leads down a sweeping mountain road before levelling out by the side of Afon Twrch.

Eventually this road leads to the B4403 at Pandy, from where it is an easy ride along the south side of Bala Lake back to the start. Alternatively you can go straight into the second circuit from this point, though be warned that it is surprisingly strength-sapping if undertaken without a break.

Second circuit

7. Follow the B4403 to Llanuwchllyn and onto the A494 where you turn right towards the Afon Lliw. After a very short distance turn left onto an unmarked lane just before the river at Pen y bont, and follow it westwards by the side of the river for just over a mile until you come to a dead-end-ahead road sign. Here you have a choice. Either turn right to Dolhendre, from where you can continue west along the road, or go straight ahead and try out the offroad option.

8. Unfortunately the offroad option has two particular problems, but it is there, it is a right of way bridleway, it should be kept open as such, and if you enjoy offroad adventure you may like to give it a go. Follow the lane straight ahead past the dead-end sign, eventually joining a track that is easily followed through to the last farmhouse, set in an isolated and very pleasant setting below Castell Carndochan. From here on the track becomes very difficult to follow. Go through the gate by the farmhouse, and then find your way along the indistinct track that keeps along the hill-

4. Continue to follow the road south across a cattle grid, entering woods at Braich-yr Owen from where there is a magical downhill that speeds you through brilliant country virtually all the way to the bridge at the northern tip of Lake Vyrnwy. Turn right here to follow the road south along the west side of the lake, and then when the road swings west turn off onto a minor road at Pont Eunant, leaving five views of this tranquil lake behind.

5. The road from Pont Eunant starts narrow

side some way above the river. It comes and goes, but when you reach a couple of boarded 'bridges' across a couple of wet sections you will know you are on the right path, eventually dropping down the hillside to cross a field to the river where you should find the bridge.

Unfortunately I found the entrance to the bridge boarded up with 'Danger – No Entry' signs, and it looked like they had been there for many a year. With no intention of turning back I found that the bridge was able to bear my weight, but there is no saying that it will do so for anyone else! (It should be repaired and put back into use by the local authority, who should also investigate why the north side is accessed by a non-bridleway stile even though it is clearly shown as bridleway by the map.) From here a left turn brings you up to the farmhouse at Buarthmeini, where a well-tied gate to the road showed that this was clearly a bridleway that gets little use; with a little sorting out it could offer a pleasant diversion.

9. From Buarthmeini the narrow road winds its way west through a fine, wild landscape that you will hopefully enjoy while meeting very few cars. Look out for the magnificent waterfall upstream from Buarthmeini, before steadily climbing uphill towards the next farmstead at Blaenlliw Isaf. Just before you reach the sheep gate here another offroad option is possible. The OS map shows a bridleway route heading due east across the hills and on through forestry before connecting with the road to the west of Parc. A member of the Rough Stuff Fellowship who was riding in the area at the same time as my visit told me that this route was reasonable to follow, but from a cursory roadside inspection it appeared likely to be lumpy, bumpy and indistinct, and probably best left for dry weather. I therefore resolved to ride on by road.

10. There does seem to be a lot of uphill along this road, before you reach the first area of forestry that scars the wilderness and signals the start of a long, fast downhill from a high point of 1,745ft (531m). With trees close on both sides, it is amazing how cold and damp it soon becomes as the pedal-turning exertion is left behind. Turn left across Pont y Gain where the road widens,

along the side of the Afon Gain, and then ride up to the next road junction where you meet the old Roman road Sarn Helen close by the remains of Roman kilns in the hillside. From the kiln area it is important to keep right, bearing round to the north on a steady uphill to follow the minor road that eventually whistles down the hillside to join to A470 close by Llyn Trawsfynydd.

11. From the A470 junction there is unfortunately no easy route off the A470 and A4212 for approximately 8 miles (13km). They are wide, fairly easy roads that pass through pleasant enough scenery and the cars should not be too much of a bother, but it is nevertheless a relief when you reach the B4391 turn-off about one mile beyond the point where you cross beneath the overhead power lines.

12. At the B4391 turn-off, ignore the signs for Bala, which is straight ahead for motor traffic, and take great care while turning right onto the minor road that is signposted for the hamlet of Llidiardau. This follows a fairly easy up and down route along the hillsides, passing close by Llyn Celyn with the remains of the railway that has secretly followed all the way along the A4212 particularly well preserved here. It stretches all the way to Bala, and would be ideal for a future cycle track in the area. Past Llidiardau the road widens and becomes less strenuous to ride, as you travel through tranquil countryside before eventually joining the A4212 for a short and easy ride into Bala.

Places To Visit:
Bala Lake Railway along the south shore of Lake Bala;
Ffestiniog Railway from Blaenau Ffestiniog to Porthmadog.

Pubs and Cafés:
Pubs and cafés at Bala;
pubs along the route at Llanuwchllyn and Trawsfynydd.

23 Round Gwydyr Forest

Mainly Offroad

Area: Snowdonia – a double circuit of the Gwydyr forest to the north and south of the A5. Start and finish at Betws-y-coed.

OS Map: OS Map: Landranger 115 – Snowdon & surrounding area.

Route:
First circuit
Betws-y-coed car park (GR:795565)
Coed Diosgydd (GR:786569)
Parc Uchaf Gwydyr (GR:795595)
Parc mine (GR:790603)
Hafna mine (GR:781601)
Bwlch-yr-haiarn (GR:773600)
Llyn y Sarnau (GR:778591)
Llyn Goddionduon (GR:754583)
Diosgydd (GR:772579)
Coed Diosgydd (GR:786569)
Betws-y-coed car park (GR:795565)
Second circuit
Betws-y-coed car park (GR:795565)
Pentre-du car park (GR:779569)
Rhiwddolion/Sarn Helen (GR:773562)
Clogwyn-brith (GR:796542)
Coed-y-celyn (GR:797552)
Betws-y-coed (GR:795565)
Extension
A470/Pont-y-pant/Sarn Helen (GR:753538)

Nearest BR Station:
Betws-y-coed.

Nearest Youth Hostel: Lledr Valley (tel: 016906 202) on the A470 close by Sarn Helen at GR:749534; Capel Curig (tel: 01690 720225) on the A5 at GR:726579.

Approx Length: First circuit 12^1/$_2$ miles (20km); second circuit 7 miles (11km) or 13 miles (21km) including the A470/Sarn Helen extension.

Time: Allow 2 hours for the first circuit; allow 1 hour for the second circuit, or 2 hours with extension.

Rating: Moderate. With the official Gwydyr trail guide there are no excuses for getting lost and the tracks are made for fast riding, but there are still plenty of hills to contend with.

The popular town of Betws-y-coed is dominated by the huge Gwydyr Forest Park, which boasts two mountain bike trails giving 20 miles (32km) or so of mainly offroad riding. The two trails can be linked together, and for extra interest there is a possible extension making use of Ride 24 and the ancient Sarn Helen road, which runs through the forest.

1. The main car park in Betws-y-coed is free, but is likely to get very crowded in the holiday season. It is conveniently close to the Y Stablau Forest Information Centre, and they will sell you a route map of the forest, which acts as a permit for using its trails. The map is reasonable value, much easier to navigate by than the OS map, and is recommended. With this in your hand you will not need a guide to each route here, but it is worth mentioning some of the high and low points of the trails.

2. To get onto the longer northern trail (first circuit), follow the A5 for a short way through Betws-y-coed before turning right over the bridge on the B5106. Immediately turn left by a small car park, and follow the narrow lane uphill in the same direction as the river, towards the first turn-off at Coed Diosgydd.

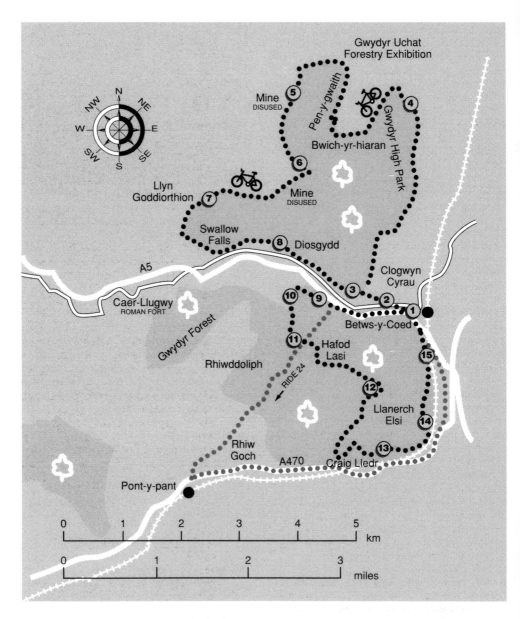

3. It is important to get things right from the start. This route is signposted for use in an anticlockwise direction, and if you attempt to ride it clockwise you will find that all the signs are the wrong way round, which makes navigation a little slower than it might be. Furthermore it must be safer if everyone travels in the same direction. You can get up a good speed on forestry tracks, and meeting someone head-on coming the other way round a bend should be avoided. So, follow the sign and turn right up the hill. It is a very steep climb on tarmac, but it soon brings you onto level high ground and forestry roads, which from here on are virtually all smooth, wide and as fast as you want to make them. It is a case of plodding or powering up each hill, depending on your inclination and fitness, and freewheeling or powering down the other side. There are a lot of similar tracks, and with so much forestry they do get a touch tedious.

4–8. At Gwydyr Uchaf the trail follows a track on an open ridge above Gwydir Castle, crossing an isolated road by some splendid old mine workings near Hafna that are well worth investigating, and then continuing in a loop past Llyn Glangors (5). From here it drops back down to the same road near Llyn y Sarnau, passing the Cyffty mine (6) where there is an interesting information board, before a final circuit of the forest roads passes close to Llyn Goddionduon (7) with some good views of the Snowdon mountains to the west. The route finally heads westwards, dropping downhill on one of the roughest tracks of the trail to rejoin the road just south of Ty'n Llwyn (8) from where it is an easy pedal back to Betws-y-coed.

9. You may like to go straight into the mountain bike trail south of the A5 (second circuit), which starts about a mile out of the centre of Betws-y-coed at Pentre-du just before the A5 passes the last buildings on the left. Here there is a small, rather hidden car park a short way up the hill, and the mountain bike route continues up through some pleasant mixed woodland with plenty of broad-leafed trees, which makes a pleasant change from the strict and very boring uniformity of the forest on the north trail.

10–14. A route sign unexpectedly takes you up a rough, tough track that is a delight after the forest uniformity, but would be much easier if ridden downhill. This leads to a more conventional forest road that takes the route across Sarn Helen at Rhiwddolion (11), and then continues on an open, fast track past the pretty Llyn Elsi reservoir (12) before following the

When the route breaks out of the forest you can get the views. Mix the route with Ride 24 and you will come up with something that is altogether more challenging.

edge of the woods above the Afon Lledr valley (13). Good views of the surrounding countryside open out at Clogwyn-brith (14), and from here there is also a not to be missed, mind-boggling descent that is super-fast as you head north to join the final road section.

11. When you hit the road by the railway bridge, a left turn will bring you back to the outskirts of Betws-y-coed. If, like I did, you fancy a little more, you could mix and match your own route option using some of Ride 24. I opted to turn right under the railway bridge, following the lane through to the A470, and from there riding the 4 miles (6km) or so to Pont-y-pant (where the Lledr Valley Youth Hostel is convenient) to join Sarn Helen and ride straight back over the top to Betws-y-coed.

Places To Visit:
Y Stablau Forest Information Centre at Betws-y-coed.

Pubs and Cafés:
Plenty of pubs and cafés at Betws-y-coed.

---

24 Old Roads from Betws-y-coed

**Offroad and
On-Road**

Area: Snowdonia – a crossing of the
hills using two ancient roads. Start and
finish at Betws-y-coed, Swallow Falls
car park or Capel Curig.

OS Map: OS Map: Landranger 115 –
Snowdon & surrounding area.

Route:
Betws-y-coed car park (GR:795565)
Swallow Falls car park/A5 (GR:760574)
A5/Caer Llugwy turn-off (GR:767575)
Chapel/old road turn-off (GR:737567)
Cefn-glas forestry (GR:732548)
Dolwyddelan/A470 (GR:738525)
A5/Pont-y-pant/Sarn Helen
(GR:753539)
Rhiwddolion/Sarn Helen (GR:773562)
A5/Miners bridge (GR:779569)
Betws-y-coed (GR:795565)

Nearest BR Station: Betws-y-coed.

Nearest Youth Hostel: Lledr Valley on
the A470 close by Sarn Helen at
GR:749534; Capel Curig on the A5 at
GR:726579.

Approx Length: 11 miles (18km).

Time: Allow 2 hours.

Rating: Moderate. Be prepared for
some technical uphill and downhill
'rockery' on both the old roads.

*The Snowdonia National Park is not par-
ticularly well endowed with bridleways,
and some of those that exist are under too
much pressure of over-use (see Ride 25).
To help mountain bikers find their way the
Park authorities have produced a map
showing all the recommended mountain
bike routes in the area, including two old
roads that do not even rate as bridleways –
the Capel Curig to Dolwyddelan road and
a nearby section of the ancient Sarn Helen.
This route explores their delights.*

1. You could start this ride from Betws-y-
coed, or from the Swallow Falls car park or one
farther to the west. Ride west along the A5 until
you come to a sharp right-hand bend in the
road about half a mile (800m) past Swallow
Falls, and here go straight ahead on a lane without a signpost.

2. This lane offers a very pretty ride, following
the side of the fast flowing river through trees
and well protected form the busy A5. After just
over a mile, look out for a footpath ladder leading down to the river. A short way on you will
see a chapel next to a small house up in the
trees to the left. Turn up by the side of the
chapel here by a footpath sign, and go through a
gate by a large notice telling you to stick to the
'road'.

3. This is the start of the old road, and at first
it is dire. It heads up the side of the hill by a
very pretty stream, but the surface is a mass of
broken rock, which makes riding a technical feat
for at least the first 800 yards. Do not worry;
once you are on the top it gets better, with the
surface much improved as the views open out
and you pass the quarry road with signs telling
you that the quarry is not the way to go.

4. The road is fairly easy to follow and ridable
all the way as it heads south towards the big
mountains in the distance, passing through a
few gates on the way. As you start to drop
downhill you will see a mass of forestry ahead,
and soon pick up a forestry road on its perimeter. Turn left here to continue riding south,

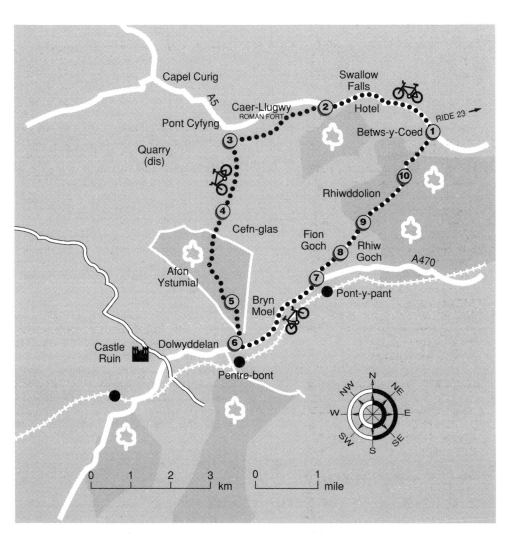

and head straight on down through the forestry, which despite the wide 'roads' can be muddy in areas where they have been logging.

5. It is easy to overshoot the correct route down to the village of Dolwyddelan on the A470. As you head down on the final stages on a fast, forest road, it curves round to the left through a triangular, yellow-painted gate just past a double footpath sign, eventually leading down to the A470 further to the east by a petrol station. Here you should bear right on a less distinct, much narrower track, and then just before you reach a cattle grid and open ground turn left down an even narrower, moderately rough track that heads down the hillside with walls on either side.

6. This brings you out to the village of Dolwyddelan conveniently close by the pub. If you want to explore farther, the ruined Dolwyddelan Castle is less than a mile along the A470 to

Crunch-crunch-crunch. Some of the old road is pretty devilish, but rest assured things can only get better.

the west. It is in a fine position and well worth a tour.

7. To continue the ride, head east along the A470, which is a relatively pleasant road. Ride past the Lledr Valley Youth Hostel, and a short way on look for a narrow lane heading left up the hill by the side of a house named Ty Sarn. This is the start of the of the few remaining sections of the ancient road Sarn Helen.

8. Ride steeply up past a few houses, going through a gate and joining a rough track by the last farmsteads near the top of the hill. Sarn Helen heads on up a track that is easy to follow, and then crosses open high ground with fine views of the mountains behind before you enter the Gwydyr forest.

9. The most important thing to remember with an old road such as Sarn Helen is that it keeps going as straight as it can. Thankfully the forestry planters have not obliterated it in this area, and at the first junction you cross over and keep in the same direction, following a narrow track that then starts to weave down the hillside between old stone walls as it passes the few houses at Rhiwddolion.

10. Keep straight ahead at the next major forest road crossing, going through a gate to join a narrow track that heads quite steeply down through the trees on a rough, loose rock surface that offers hard technical riding. Farther down the hill the track improves, passing an isolated house and continuing downhill to emerge at the car park, which starts one of the official Gwydyr Forest Park Trails (Ride 23) close by the A5 with a short pedal back to Betws-y-coed if that is where you are headed.

Places To Visit:
Y Stablau Forest Information Centre at Betws-y-coed;
Dolwyddelan Castle (Cadw) on the A470.

Pubs and Cafés:
Plenty of pubs and cafés at Betws-y-coed;
pub at Dolwyddelan;
Plas Hall Hotel at Pont-y-pant.

---

25 In the Shadow of Snowdon

*Offroad and
On-Road*

Area: Snowdonia – a crossing of the old tracks and roads beneath the summit of Snowdon. Start and finish at Llanberis on the A4086.

OS Map: Landranger 115 – Snowdon & surrounding area.

Route:
Llanberis car park (GR:577604)
Llanberis Youth Hostel (GR:574596)
Telegraph bridleway (GR:577579)
Snowdon Ranger bridleway
(GR:573552)
Snowdon Ranger Youth Hostel/A4085
(GR:565550)
A4085/Croesywaun (GR:524593)
Groeslon (GR:527600)
Bwlch-y-Groes (GR:558599)
Llanberis car park (GR:577604)

Nearest BR Station: Bangor.

Nearest Youth Hostel:
Llanberis; Snowdon Ranger.

Approx Length: 18¹/₂ miles (30km).

Time: Allow 3 hours.

Rating: Moderate. There are some long climbs. Watch out for foul weather on the mountain sides. Be prepared to give way to all walkers.

As the result of considerable over-use the principal bridleway routes leading to the summit of Snowdon have a voluntary ban for mountain bikes from 10am to 5pm every day from 1 June to 30 September. The three routes affected are the Llanberis, Snowdon Ranger (top part) and Rhyd Ddu bridleways, and so far the voluntary ban has proved successful though if it ceases to be so a mandatory ban may well follow. In common sense terms it seems better for mountain bikers to leave the summit of Snowdon to the walkers, or at least only attempt to go up there when there are very few people about. The route that follows explores some of the lower tracks that suffer less pressure, but are still best avoided in the high season.

1. Llanberis makes a good place to start this ride from with its large, free car park close by the Power of Wales Centre, though there is also a convenient car park close to the Snowdon Ranger Youth Hostel on the A4086 side of the route. Which way to go round presents a problem, since there are very definite advantages and disadvantages to going clockwise or anticlockwise at different points of the route.

2. With the weather closing in and looking particularly menacing up on Snowdon, I opted to ride the route clockwise, getting the Telegraph bridleway section finished before the weather deteriorated any further. Leave the main road and ride up towards the big church, passing a supermarket on the corner and then turning left up a narrow road signposted to the Llanberis Youth Hostel, which is reached by keeping straight on up the hill.

3. At the Llanberis Youth Hostel keep straight on, following the narrow tarmac lane as it winds up the hillside and eventually brings you to a gate with a rough track continuing by the last house at the end of the tarmac. From here the track is easy to follow and good to ride, dipping down and then heading uphill once again as it gets closes to Snowdon, with the track eventually following the side of the valley past one

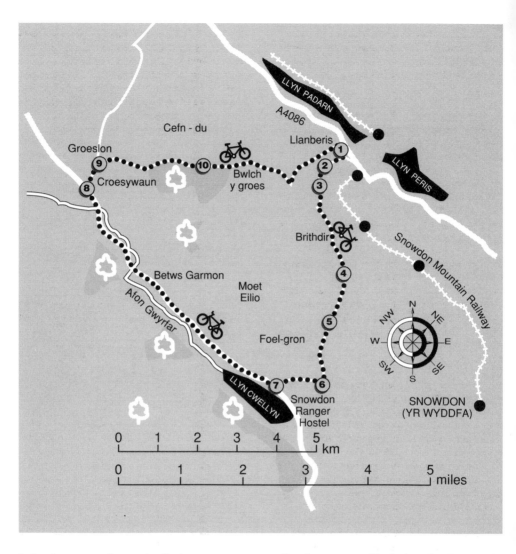

isolated cottage and a couple of ruins.

4. From here the Telegraph bridleway follows a narrow track along the hillside, heading steadily up a very long valley on its way to the top of the pass at Foel Gron. When I rode it the wind was blowing half a gale straight down this valley, which made it hard to ride and very uncomfortable. There is much to be said for riding this section downhill in the other direction: you would win here but lose on the other side.

5. At the top of the pass you can shelter and rest by a stone wall if required. Then carry on straight ahead through a gate by a footpath ladder, and follow a rough and badly eroded track down the hill on the other side to link up with the bottom section of the Snowdon Ranger bridleway, which is not subject to the voluntary ban. Keep on down the hillside with fine views opening out over Llyn Cwellyn and the mountains beyond, and you will eventually reach a junction with the Snowdon Ranger bridleway, which is a clear track.

6. Turn right down this track, and then start to follow the zigzags, which will bring you down to the A4085. This part of the route is also badly eroded, and it makes sense to wheel your bike on the most vulnerable sections to save them from abuse by your chunky tyres. On a weekend or in fine weather you can expect to meet quite a few walkers here, and should be prepared to stop and give way at every opportunity.

7. The track passes the side of a small farmhouse with a huge water-wheel, and then joins the A4085 a short distance from the Snowdon Ranger Youth Hostel. Turn right along the road here, and follow it for approximately 4 miles (6km) to the village of Croesywaun. The A4085 is easy riding, and if there are not many cars about is also quite pleasant.

8. As you cross the road bridge over the Afon Gwyrfai into Croesywaun, ignore the first right turn, which goes off to the right by a fish and chip shop, and then take the second right turn. This leads up through somewhat dreary surroundings to a crossroads at Groeslon where a signpost informs you that the way to Llanberis is straight ahead. Do not take any notice. Turn right here, following the old road that goes up over the hills on a direct route to Llanberis.

9. Ride uphill past the last terrace of houses of this grey village, bearing right at the top to join a narrow road that starts to head quite steeply up the hillside. This brings you to the top of the hills by a large patch of forestry where you leave the tarmac behind, joining a rough track that continues the road.

10. Bear right with the main track at the end of the forestry, going through a gate and then starting a long descent down the other side as the twin lakes of Llanberis – Llyn Padarn and Llyn Peris – come into view. As the track gets steeper its surface deteriorates but is still ridable, swinging in a loop to the south to come down to an isolated cottage where it once again makes contact with tarmac. From here it is a quick ride down the road into Llanberis, but watch out for the gates.

Places To Visit:
The Power of Wales Centre in Llanberis (tel: 01286 870636);
Snowdon Mountain Railway (tel: 01286 870223).

Pubs and Cafés:
Pubs and cafés at Llanberis.

Cycling Books from The Crowood Press

Great Cycle Routes – North and South Downs	Jeremy Evans
Great Cycle Routes – Dartmoor and Exmoor	Jeremy Evans
Great Cycle Routes – Dorset and the New Forest	Jeremy Evans
Great Cycle Routes – Cumbria and North Yorkshire	Jeremy Evans
Cycling on Road and Trail	Jeremy Evans
50 Mountain Bike Rides	Jeremy Evans
Offroad Adventure Cycling	Jeremy Evans
Cycling in France	Tim Hughes
Cycle Sport	Peter Konopka
Touring Bikes	Tony Oliver
Adventure Mountain Biking	Carlton Reid
Mountain Biking – The Skills of the Game	Paul Skilbeck